# INSTANT
# MENDING
## OF CHINA, POTTERY, GLASS & JEWELRY

# INSTANT MENDING

# MENDING

## OF CHINA, POTTERY, GLASS & JEWELRY

by Laurence Adams Malone,
LL.B., D.Sc.

Published by Betterway Publications, Inc.
Box 64, White Hall, VA 22987

Cover design by Julienne McNeer
Photography by Kerry Kraus and Patricia Dalzell
Illustrations by the author

Every precaution has been taken in preparing *Instant Mending of China,
Glass, Pottery, and Jewelry* to make your mending projects as safe and
successful as possible. However, neither Betterway Publications nor the
author assume any responsibility for any damages incurred in conjunction
with the use of this manual.

**Library of Congress Cataloging-in-Publication Data**

Malone, Laurence Adams.
  Instant mending of china, glass, pottery, and jewelry.

  Includes index.
  1. Pottery — Repairing.      2. Porcelain — Repairing.
  3. Glassware — Repairing.      4. Jewelry — Repairing.
  I. Title.
NK4233.M33    1986        738.1'8        86-17616
ISBN 0-932620-64-7 (pbk.)

Printed in the United States of America
0987654321

*Dedicated to*
*the creative inventor*

# CONTENTS

# INTRODUCTION: HOW TO MEND YOUR BROKEN TREASURES ... INSTANTLY

The purpose and scope of Part I of this book is to teach you quickly how to mend your broken treasure, whether it is of glass or china, with epoxies in kit form that you can buy in any hardware store, such as Krazy Glue or an ultraviolet curing glass adhesive called Crystal Clear. You will find step-by-step procedures in recipe style, with easy to follow illustrations on how to use these instant mending materials and on how to make good repairs on dinnerware, vases, lamps, dolls, boxes, figurines, heirlooms or objects of art. The mending procedures that will be given you in this section of *Instant Mending of China, Glass, Pottery, and Jewelry* are non-professional and apply only to use of instant mending materials for the non-professional.

The illustrations and instructions and the instant mending materials used cover all the different types of mends that there are, such as cracks, glaze damage, rim flake chips, and rim chips. However, this section will not go into discussion of how to make your mend invisible or how to learn highly skilled professional techniques of mending. Such techniques are set forth in the succeeding chapters of this book. This section of this mending book will show you how to make all sorts of repairs such as how to fill in a simple chip and how to use instant mending materials for instant bonding.

The point of having such a section in a mending book is to enable you to gather up all your broken pieces, quickly put them together for safekeeping and preservation, and to restore the article to immediate use, if necessary. The book is set up especially in cook-book recipe style to make it easy for you to find the right mending recipe immediately and by using the right instant mending material, to mend the broken piece you have on hand.

**Note:** The use of miracle-mending materials described in this book and used according to the step-by-step procedures outlined, together with the increasing skill and experience of a mender, will generally produce miracle results. Some mending can be invisibilized and the mended article restored to normal use. Occasionally, however, a mender discovers that the materials and techniques that have produced perfect results time and again on articles of china, glass, and pottery may *not* produce the same results with other articles that appear to be similar.

The cause of this problem may be in the composition, age, or source of the article. A wide variety of materials from the earth are used in a variety of combinations in making different kinds of articles of china, glass, and pottery. For example, glass may contain lead, lime, or silver, and some of the compounds in glassware may be nonresponsive to mending materials, while apparently similar articles may be easily and perfectly mended.

Occasionally, there *is* an element of chance that must be taken into account in mending. The flaw or fault may be inherent in the composition of the article itself, rather than in the mending materials or the careful skill of the mender.

Laurence Adams Malone

# PART I

# CHAPTER ONE: A SYSTEM OF INSTANT MENDING FOR NON-PROFESSIONALS

I nstant china and glass mending instruction is based on use of instant mending materials, available in almost any hardware store.

The instruction is professional. The results will be your own. There is no guarantee that instant mending materials will even do the job you have to do, nor is there any guarantee that the mended piece will hold together in water, or if left in a damp place that it will continue to hold together. Many mended articles of either glass or chinaware (such as a Corning ware casserole) when mended with instant mending materials will come apart if subjected to heat in an oven. If the casserole has been mended and is holding together fairly well, do not use it in your oven. Try cooking in another container and pour or transfer the food to the casserole after the cooking is done. It may stand the heat of the food, but it will not stand the heat of the oven above 250 degrees. Nor will it stand such temperature for more than a few minutes.

The instructions given in this book will tell you how best to use instant mending materials and how to put the broken pieces together on an instant bonding basis.

There are three words that have been used frequently in relation to mending chinaware and glassware. These words refer to a way in which mending materials are used. These are mend, repair, and restore.

With the proper System, the materials are used:

> To mend a break
> To repair a damage
> To restore a missing part

If you understand the way in which each term is used following the step-by-step sequences will be easier.

And that is what this part of the book is all about, making it easier for you to use instant mending materials.

**Missing pieces.** A missing piece or missing pieces from a broken piece of chinaware can only be replaced by using the putty clay material and by following the professional instructions given in preceding chapters of this book. A missing piece of glass may be restored by using an instant mending material called Crystal Clear.

One may use an instant mending material such as Krazy Glue to very quickly piece together all the broken pieces. One advantage in using such a material is that it takes but a few minutes. However, you must have skillful, nimble fingers and avoid getting any of this material on your fingers as it will instantly bond your fingers together. And it will be very unpleasant getting them apart, unless you immediately dip them into some handy solvent such as Acetone or lacquer thinner. And even then the experience will be unpleasant. Many people are quite skillful with their hands and would find this no drawback. Also, using Krazy Glue yields the advantage that it will preserve the broken article until it can be done professionally without risk of loss of any of the pieces.

**Mending broken glass.** The same reasoning applies. If you have chipped your fine drinking or wine glasses, you will not find anyone who will grind down the chipped edges. So you will be faced with replacement of the article or instant mending. Many antique dealers unpacking for an Antique Show have unfortunately chipped a precious glass at the last moment before the show opens. They usually carry the instant mending material called Crystal Clear, as it needs only be applied and set in a sunny spot to heal the break in a matter of 10 seconds.

## Cautionary Information
## About Mending Materials

The instant mending materials listed for use in this section of this book are high tech, sophisticated chemical compounds and should be used with considerable caution. Keep all materials out of the reach of children. Before using such materials, please take a minute to read the information given on the label. All epoxy resins may cause an allergic skin reaction. Provide adequate ventilation and avoid prolonged breathing of any vapor rising from any of the cyanoacrylic bonding adhesives. Wash hands with soap and water after using. In case of contact with skin or eyes, flush with plenty of water and, if necessary, do not hesitate to call a physician or get to an emergency room at your nearest hospital.

Keep all instant mending materials away from heat, sparks or an open or glowing flame such as a cigarette. Recap your mending materials when not in use.

All repaired articles should be carefully washed with soap and water after full curing time has been allowed. Full curing time is usually given on the card or under directions for use on the label.

# CHAPTER TWO: STUDY THE BROKEN ARTICLE, SET UP A SMALL WORK AREA AND BEGIN . . .

I n every home, treasures or simply useful articles of china and glass are frequently broken. These need not always be discarded. With the instructions given in this book for quick and easy mending, and a supply of relatively inexpensive mending materials ($1.98 to $10.00 at the most), broken articles of china and glass can be restored to their original usefulness.

## SETTING UP A WORK AREA

An ordinary enamel top kitchen table will do. Good light is very important. Examine the list of basic quick and easy mending materials, page 23–27, and the kind of a mending job you have on hand, page 20–21, to determine exactly the mending material you will need to do the job, quickly and easily. You may want to keep a small section of a cupboard where you can store your mending materials in a cigar box, as such materials may come in handy for mending jobs from time to time and most of them can be used again and again. Also, supply yourself with a second cigar box full of white sand, as you will need this sand box in which to up-end and balance articles that you mend. The sand box will permit you to balance your articles at all sorts of crazy angles, even down side up. And you will find this a very important asset when you apply your mending techniques.

## STUDY THE BROKEN ARTICLE

Let us begin with a broken china cup or saucer or a piece of pottery. What kind of chinaware is it? Or what kind of pottery is it? You will need to know if either of these two kinds of ware are hard or soft, porous or nonporous, in order to select the right kind of instant mending material.

All chinaware, as well as stoneware, pottery, and any other product of ceramic art, is fashioned of clay, except compo pieces. Compo pieces can be made of soft, easily broken material such as Plaster of Paris. Such pieces of ware, while they may be highly decorative and ornamental, are very porous and instant mending materials will not work to mend them. The pieces cannot be cemented together as the porous plaster or soft claylike material simply absorbs the material when applied and the pieces will not adhere to one another.

*Set up a home work area with a workbench and a supply of relatively inexpensive mending materials*

# CHAPTER THREE:
# SECRETS OF MENDING CHINA, PORCELAIN, STONEWARE, POTTERY, AND GLASSWARE

In mending a piece of broken china, you will learn some of the secrets of clay. Some of the recommended mending materials have a resinous or adhesive base, some a cyanoacrylate base, still others have a methacrylic ester base and are highly adhesive on nonporous surfaces. As you work with broken articles to mend, you will learn about the hardness and porousness of the piece, the quality of its surface and how quickly to mend it.

**Chinaware** is usually made of clay. Clay is formed by the decomposition of rock. There are different kinds of clay because there are different kinds of rock, and from different kinds of clay we have different kinds of china, varying in quality, hardness, usefulness, and beauty. The main ingredient of all chinaware clay is a kind of sand called silicon. This is a glassy, non-metallic resinous sand which makes up more than half the earth's crust. When combined with oxygen, silicon makes silica, which is used to make glassware. Another essential part of all clay is alumina. When silica and alumina are combined with kaolin, which is a very fine, white clay, ball clay is formed, from which china can be produced. Ball clay fires white and has fine texture, quality, and hardness. It is used principally to make porcelain and white ware ceramic objects such as fine dinnerware, decorative accessories and objects of art. Other kinds of clay are used to make brick, furnace linings, stoneware, and pottery and other ceramics.

With this information in mind, let's examine the piece of china to be mended. Is it in several pieces or merely cracked? Is it made of porcelain or of a vitreous composition, that is full of ground glass? Are any pieces missing? Has it been mended earlier?

Suppose you have a china cup, broken in several pieces, and previously mended. The first step is to boil the article to get all the pieces apart and have them thoroughly clean and free of old cement before working on them to repair both the old and new damage. Getting the old glue off is necessary with any broken article, whether glass or china. Before doing any cementing, the surface to be recemented or repaired must be *truly clean.* Boiling also takes out any dirt that has seeped into cracks and any discoloration.

For boiling, use a white enamel dishpan or small bucket, covering the article well in almost pure Clorox. The Clorox will not take off any gold paint or colored decoration that is original to the piece and that has been baked on or fired in its manufacture. But Clorox will severely corrode a container made of galvanized metal or aluminum. The same boiling and bleaching process is used to restore to almost original brilliance an item on which a million tiny cracks appear in the glaze. Surface damage such as this is referred to as "crazed," and even when this occurs, boiling in Clorox will not harm the original painted decoration under the glaze. As soon as the article is thoroughly bleached and clean, wrap each piece in Saran or other transparent material to keep it dust-free until you are ready to work on it.

If the item is a broken cup and it is now in several pieces, you should understand that every piece you cement together is going to be slightly larger because of the mending material added to it. Thus, the material between several pieces cemented together is going to cause some displacement.

It is at this point that sandpaper is useful to smooth away the roughness of the final edges of the last piece to fit in. For beginners, when the displacement is minimal, sanding down with garnet paper may be sufficient. If you decide that the piece you have selected is too badly broken for inexperienced mending and you do not have a handgrinder, why not wrap the pieces carefully and keep them. The time may come more quickly than you suspect when skill, materials, and equipment will enable you to do the job after all.

For the moment, let us examine a broken piece of china —your cup. This is important because its texture and hardness, coarseness or fineness, thickness or thinness is going to determine the mending materials needed to make an invisible repair.

Is it earthenware? This is rather flaky, soft, and porous and one might be almost held together by glaze. Dig at the edges with fingernail or sharp instrument. Earthenware gives way and chips off quite easily. The color is usually tan or reddish or white.

**Porcelain** (china) on the other hand, requires high temperature firing and comes out as the finest of all ceramic artware. It is a hard vitreous Kaolin clay that fires to a translucent jewel-like white, sparkling, lustrous and beautiful. Antique figurines and dinnerware made of porcelain (ball clay) are highly prized by collectors throughout the world. Any objects made of porcelain are indeed worth repairing with painstaking care. You will however, be working as a ceramist does, with basic natural clay, but with mending materials such as Porcelainate Powder and Hardener, with perhaps epoxies and resins made to produce good mending results to simulate the lustrous porcelain-like finish the article had before being damaged.

**Stoneware** is different from earthenware and porcelain (china). It has a hard, glassy, vitreous body, frequently called ironstone. The two words glassy and vitreous together call attention to the nature of vitreous porcelain-like texture. Some kinds of stoneware are best mended with the same materials used to mend glassware. They are that glassy. If the texture glitters like granite, the name graniteware is often given to an article. When pieces of stoneware are fired, they first turn to varying shades of gray or brown. A mixture of firebrick clay produces the rough texture from which stoneware gets its name.

**Pottery,** which may also be called earthenware, is made of coarse clay hardened by heat. It is merely a firm but pliable kind of earth, a clay containing kaolin, which can be easily molded, shaped, fired, and hardened for commercial use.

Stoneage man made his utensils of clay. These were not fired, but as primitive peoples learned that fire made the clay harder and they developed crude methods of firing, pottery making became a handcraft.

The Chinese learned how to shape, decorate, glaze, and adulterate pottery, and as early as 206 B.C. were making beautiful pieces of "bronzed" types of jars, pots, and mugs. About a thousand years later, we have examples of the finest Chinese ceramics, and for the first time we see the so-called stoneware. This type of pottery is made of hard, dense clay mixed with silica, then fired at high temperatures to produce a tight, granite-like substance, non-porous and highly susceptible to beautiful glazing. In the latter half of the 15th century, glazed pottery was given the name Faience when the town of Faeriza in Italy began to make some of the most beautiful majolica the world has ever seen. Delftware, majolica, slipware, and faience are all basically pottery, and all such pottery is porous, requiring epoxy for a good repair job.

Now you know why it is necessary to know something about the composition of an article before the work of mending is started.

**Glass** is recognized by everyone. It is hard and brittle, smooth to the touch, and delightful to the eye. Although other ingredients may be added, the fundamental ones are silica, soda, lime and often potash. Certainly nature melted sand and soda into glass long before man appeared; but there is evidence of man's having created objects of glass as far back as the year 12,000 B.C. In the Corning Museum in Corning, New York, there is a string of beads, some ceramic, others with solid glass, dating to the year 1500 B.C. Today, glass is produced of sand, boric oxidem lead or silver, sometimes gold, calcium or lime, sodium and potassium oxides.

Nearly everyone owns three types of glass.

1. Soda-lime glass, used in making bottles.
2. Lead glass, used for tableware.
3. Boro-silicate glass, used for ovenware.

Another type of glass is crystal. Antique crystal ware from the 17th and 18th centuries was made from flintstones rather than sand. Flintstone is used to describe a beautiful, colorless glassware that can be made to sound with a bell-like ring.

Glass tableware and crystal articles used as decorative accessories are pieces that most often need and are worth mending.

You will be startled to learn that the transparence and brilliancy of your most beautiful glassware is achieved and enhanced by the use of arsenic! But never mind, you will not need arsenic to mend your broken glass.

As in the case of mending china, examine the damaged article very carefully and classify the damage under the headings as listed for china (e.g., chips, flake chips, broken out pieces, missing pieces, multiple breaks, fractures or cracks, hairline cracks and "spider-spreader" types of cracks.

For all articles made of glass, you will use a clear epoxy and resin mixture that produces a self-hardening adhesive. It does not depend upon heat or air for drying. This cement forms into a tight joining substance that is unaffected by alcohol and hot and cold water. When used according to the instructions given in this book, the joint or mend should never come apart.

This adhesive may also be used to bond together other types of broken articles such as chinaware.

You may be ready at this point to turn to the index and locate the instructions for the particular type of repair job that is needed to mend your article. There are recipes, much as one would find in a good cook book, for nearly every type of mending job you might need to do. For many jobs, you may need to read two or three recipes — for instance, cup with broken handle, cup with bad crack, and cup with lip piece missing.

Let us examine for a moment the different kinds of mending jobs, anyone of which you may have to do.

# DIFFERENT KINDS OF MENDING JOBS

1. A small surface flake damage to the glaze.
2. A surface flake that is called a chip, which includes glaze damage.

3. A chip that is out of an edge or one that is called a "lip chip" such as the edge of a drinking vessel, cup or glass. "Edge chip" would be applied to a saucer or plate or the edge of any object to which we do not put our lips.
4. A broken out piece.
5. An article broken in two or more places, such as a vase or a lamp.
6. A broken base or pedestal.
7. A broken lid.
8. A broken finial to a lid.
9. A broken spout
10. A broken handle.
11. Hairline crack.
12. Missing parts, such as heads, hands, legs, feet, wings, leaf, flowers, fruit, finials, knobs, handles, spouts, lids, and perhaps others too similar to mention.

Now when you have examined the article to be mended and are familiar with the materials of which it is made and have determined what type of mending is necessary, your next question is, "What materials and supplies will I need to start mending?"

## Different Kinds of Mending Jobs

*Glaze damage.*

*A surface chip, sometimes called a flake chip or edge chip.*

*Damage to the edge called a lip chip.*

*Note:* Remove old material from any article that has been previously mended.

# CHAPTER FOUR: INSTANT MENDING MATERIALS: WHAT THEY ARE AND WHERE TO FIND THEM

H igh technology has provided us, today, with general purpose adhesives that will handle almost any household mending project. These adhesive products are obtainable at any hardware or art supply store.

The list of adhesive products given below are water resistant and are specifically designated because they will bond glass, ceramics, and most other materials.

In most instances, you will discover in working with these products that you have unlimited working time UNTIL you press the two parts together that are to be mended, then you will find that the mending material will bond the broken pieces together in about 30-45 seconds. Some of these products will also bond to your skin, so a note of caution is suggested as the bond to your skin can be instantaneous and can only be dissolved by immediately dipping your fingers into a solvent liquid such as nail polish remover, which is otherwise known as Acetone. Or if you have some Lacquer Thinner on hand, you may use the lacquer thinner to dissolve the bond. Either of these two solvents will also undo a badly done mending job and enable you to start over.

## FOR MENDING BROKEN CHINAWARE

**Depend II** — Locktite Corporation Product

**Master Mend** — An E Pox E System; Locktite

**E Pox E Glue** — Bonds glass and ceramics permanently. It is transparent and waterproof, and a Locktite Corporation Product

**Seal All** — Also works on Stoneware and Pottery. Allen Products Corp.

**Adhesive** — Dow Corning Corp. Product

**Super Glue** — Locktite Corporation Product. Not recommended for use on Glass. Also will bond to your skin, see note of caution above

**Stix All** — A Borden Product. Will not bond to your fingers and dries clear. StixAll is highly resistant to water and can be used to mend porous materials such as cookery or soft clay pottery

# FOR MENDING GLASSWARE

**Crystal Clear** — An ultraviolet glass adhesive that cures in the sunlight. Crystal clear glass adhesive has the same clarity as glass, providing an invisible bond line. Exposure to daylight (ultraviolet rays) to cure in seconds. Only the adhesive in the bond area will cure: any excess easily wipes away. Can be used for stained glass (not opaque) and bonding metal to glass. Perfect for repairing fine glassware, serving-ware, and crystal. Crystal Clear Glass Adhesive's rapid bonding action is triggered by ultraviolet light which is present in natural daylight. In strong sunlight a clear bond is formed in about 10 seconds — on a dull or cloudy day allow about 1 to 2 minutes.

**Master Mend** — This Locktite product requires extra working time and only works on glass according to the particular code of the E Pox E system indicated on the product card. You cannot simply walk into the hardware store and buy just any card labeled E Pox E system. The proper card for glass will be coded by color and given a number, such as 70Blue.

However, bear in mind that this system combines the convenience of extra working time and application versatility.

**E Pox E Glue** — This epoxy product is useful for an extra strong bond. It is transparent and water proof. It is a Resin and Hardener (in equal quantities) and must be thoroughly mixed for use. Once thoroughly cured, E Pox E Glue is not effected by water, naptha, or any thinner or solvent. Bear in mind you will have to go to considerable trouble to undo a bad mending job, as the usual solvents will not work. Instructions on how to undo badly done work will be given to you in the directions on how to use your mending materials, elsewhere detailed in this book.

**Seal All** — This material is again mentioned here as it may be used to good advantage on glass and for general purpose use.

**Adhesive** — This Dow Corning product takes about 5 minutes to work, and fully cures in about 24 hours. It is highly water resistant.

**"Touch-n-Glue" Weldwood** — This product is put out by the Roberts Consolidated Industries and is a fine bonding product for glass and general purpose use. Fast bonding occurs. The product is strong and resilient and nonflammable.

# FOR MENDING JEWELRY

**Adhesive** — A Dow Corning product, this adhesive works well on jewelry mending as one can achieve a three dimensional effect.

# OTHER PRODUCTS AND MANUFACTURERS

**Silicone Adhesive/Sealant** — Dow Corning Product.

**Permabond 102** — Pearl Chemical Company.

**Elmer's Acrylic Latex** — Borden product. This product cannot be dissolved with lacquer thinner as it is a latex base product.

**Elmer's China-Glass Cement** — Also a Borden latex base product.

**Krazy Glue** — Krazy Glue, Inc. An instant bonding material. This product can be dissolved with lacquer thinner or Acetone and it is recommended that you work with thinner ready at hand when you use this material.

**Kay-O-Lin** — An epoxybond resin and hardener. This two part china clay mending product is distributed through hardware stores, in kits, by Atlas Mineral & Chemical Company (Mertztown, PA 19539) under the name Epoxy Bond Resin and Epoxy Bond Hardener, or it may be obtained by writing to the author at 2111 Jefferson Davis Hwy., Arlington, VA 22202. This system is the only one known to the author that can be used to fill in missing chipped out pieces of broken chinaware, as well as missing pieces. It is especially useful as a filler where surface and edge damages occur to broken articles of chinaware. It also forms a permanent bond for putting on broken handles, and for covering over unsightly damaged and cracked areas.

**New Gloss Glaze** — This is a glaze coating material patented and produced by the author. It is distributed through hardware stores by Atlas Mineral & Chemical Company or may be obtained by writing to the author.

# INSTANT MENDING MATERIALS

**Krazy Glue**. — Krazy Glue is an eye irritant and must be used with extreme caution as it bonds skin instantly. To avoid the unpleasant effects of this mending material you should have some acetone on hand in a little pot or dish so that you can immediately dip your fingers into the acetone to wipe off any Krazy Glue.

Krazy Glue itself contains cyanoacrylate, which is an immediate bonding or adhesive material. Its affect if you get a drop of it on your skin or fingers is to make your fingers stick together. If skin bonding occurs, dip your fingers immediately in acetone or nail polish remover and the Krazy Glue will be diluted and dissipate leaving your fingers free. Krazy Glue may be used to piece together broken pieces of chinaware, ironstone, porcelain ware, and in some instances it may be used successfully in mending cut glass. Krazy Glue will not bond pottery because pottery is too porous. The same is true of composition type chinaware, sometimes called faience or soft paste. You will be able to tell what composition your chinaware consists of by testing a broken edge with the sharp point of a knife. If it is chalky, Krazy Glue will not do the mending job nor will any other instant mending material such as Duco cement or Elmer's glue. Soft paste pieces of chinaware once broken will have to be mended using professional techniques set forth in the preceding chapters of this book.

**Sunshine Glass-Glue.** — Sunshine glass glue repairs broken glass in ten seconds flat with sun power. Silicic science has combined the power of sunshine with ultraviolet curing molecules to produce an invisible glue for glass and fine crystal. The chemical reaction takes place in ten seconds in sunlight. Perhaps a minute or more on a cloudy day. With Sunshine Glass Glue you can mend the most priceless crystal as well as colored glass like stained glass. Use may apply to every type of broken glassware except opaque types. You can even repair chips and voids that often appear in glassware. No matter what the breakage problem, whether for practical or cosmetic purposes, Sunshine Glass Glue may be just the answer as it does what no bonding agent has ever accomplished. After application of the substance to the broken article, you simply put it in the sunshine coming through your window for a few minutes. The mend will have taken place, the breaks will be healed and you simply wipe off the excess. Your article may also be washed.

Sunshine Glass-Glue sometimes is labeled Crystal Clear. It is a Duro product manufactured by the Locktite Corporation and should be available from your local hardware store.

# CHAPTER FIVE:
# HOW TO USE INSTANT
# MENDING MATERIALS

T he kit of material, whether a single adhesive or a resin and hardener system will not include all the materials you need for mending chinaware, table service pieces, decorative accessories, fine porcelains, glass stoneware, and pottery.

Mending any broken article of value is worth the time and effort required to do a good job. The best mending material for that job must be determined by your careful attention to what is in the kit. You must also have a small but adequate work area set up, with good light and air.

The following list refers to materials suitable for making repairs and obtaining the best results in the shortest time possible. The first step is to become familiar with these various mending materials and to learn what each one will do. The process is selective when it comes to instant mending materials, as you may be entirely inexperienced, hesitant, or your approach may be to use a material that gives you more mending time than an instant bond. Instant bond material such as Krazy Glue may work entirely too quickly for your personal comfort. You may prefer to work with a resin and hardener type mending kit which would allow you unlimited preparation time and take longer to cure. If you are very slow and cautious about doing perfect work the first time around, then perhaps the slower approach is the better approach for you. All of the resin and hardener two-part systems are characterized by toughness, strong adhesion, and high corrosion resistance. They are different from glue, which is generally the product of boiling together the bones, cartilage, and connective tissue of animals. Epoxy produces an adhesive. Broken articles that are epoxybonded become whole again. Articles mended with epoxybond resin will not come apart easily although almost all instant mending materials will not stand up under dishwasher treatment. Most mending materials will come apart when subjected to boiling, or in water brought to a boiling hot temperature.

When you are ready to use instant mending material to bond your broken article, you will want certain equipment on hand in the area you have set aside for your mending job.

The equipment recommended for use in all step-by-step sequences given for instant mending specific articles of china (Chapter 7), glass (Chapter 8), and pottery (Chapter 9), or jewelry (Chapter 10) is, as follows:

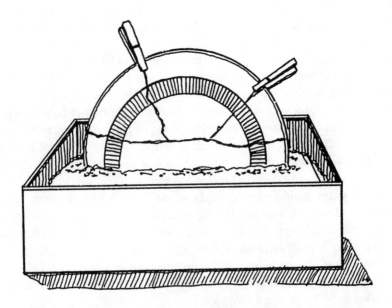

*Supply yourself with a sturdy box large enough to hold a bed of white sand.*
*As illustrated by the plate in the sandbox, the lower half is bearing the weight of the upper pieces that are cemented in place and held by wooden clamp-type clothespins. The four edges have been cemented in a balanced position, and the entire plate is then placed on its lower edge deep in the sandbox for balance.*

# EQUIPMENT

**Brushes** — Three or four, of varying size and thickness, (obtained from any art supply store). Acrylic bristle brushes with unpainted wooden handles are preferred.

**Razor blades** — Single edge, for trimming away excess materials.

**Small saucer** — Of china or glass (never plastic), for use in mixing various two part system materials. A curved saucer about 3 inches in diameter is excellent for runny, or syrupy-type cements that go through a thickening stage before becoming a workable adhesive.

**Wipers** — Either paper napkins or paper towels, in handy packets. Cheese cloth cut in convenient small squares is also useful for this purpose.

**Apron** — A workman's apron is excellent, and should be large enough to protect clothing, as drops of instant mending materials may fall unnoticed onto your clothing and are not removable once they harden.

**Lacquer thinner** — For small mending jobs that can be done quickly, you will always need a small quantity of solvent such as nail polish remover, or lacquer thinner, to help wipe away excess and to use to protect your fingers in case the bonding material bonds to your skin.

**Sandbox** — Any sturdy box (a cake tin) large enough to hold a bed of white sand (which you can get at any pet shop) will help you immeasurably. Especially when you have to do a mending job that requires that the article be balanced at an unusual angle. You will want a depth of 3 to 4 inches of sand. Articles that are being mended can be propped in the sandbox while curing is in progress. If the article is heavy, tongue depressors can support it in the sand. After use, you may wish to put back the sand in the heavy bag in which you bought it and simply store for future use in your work area.

**Metal waste basket** — Never plastic. For catching all debris quickly.

**Scotch tape** — This serves the same general purpose as masking tape. So you may use masking tape rather than scotch tape if you prefer or find it easier to work with.

**Small glass pot** — For holding water or thinner (acetone).

# CHAPTER SIX:
# IS IT WORTH MENDING?

## DETERMINE THE VALUE OF THE ARTICLE TO BE MENDED

1. Determine whether the damaged article is worth the time and the relatively small cost of mending materials. If the article can be easily and inexpensively replaced, that is one matter. If it belongs to a table service or a set or a pair, and cannot be replaced, mend it. If the article has sentimental value to you or is a piece of intrinsic value and beauty, by all means mend it. (Visiting antique shops and attending antique shows, or researching the table of marks that appears in the Appendix, may provide some pleasant surprises about the increasing value of old china). The decision about mending is up to you.

2. Study the broken or damaged article carefully. It may be helpful, at first, for you to make a list on paper of the damages: flake, surface flake or chip, edge or lip chip, missing piece or pieces, cracks and fractures, broken off handles, spouts, finials, and knobs. Do you have them, whole or broken, or have they been lost?

3. Decide on the order in which these damages are to be repaired. How much can you do at one sitting using the same mix? Time can be saved if you have several pieces of china to be repaired (such as several plates, saucers, cups, and other pieces of a table service, with similar damages on each piece) and can work on all the pieces at one work session. Remember that adequate time for drying and hardening of mending materials must be allowed.

4. Select the proper instant mending materials as recommended for each type of damage.

# A BRIEF HISTORY OF
# CHINAWARE AND PORCELAIN

The name comes from China where the product was first made many centuries ago — perhaps as early as 206 B.C. to 220 A.D. — definitely a flourishing business by the ninth and tenth centuries. Chinaware is characteristic of a cultural heritage and a love of beauty that is centuries older than that of European countries.

From the beginning, chinaware was made of two earth substances, petuntse and kaolin, made by crushing granite rock (felsite) until, with the addition of water, the mass attains the consistency of clay. The basic differences between the two is that quartz, which forms a considerable part of petuntse, is not present in kaolin. When these two clays are mixed, they reinforce each other. The kaolin makes the mixture more easily molded and modeled. Because of its quartz content, petuntse fuses with the mixture completely to form the hard, glassy, translucent surface that is characteristic of "true" porcelain. If broken, the break in the porcelain article will show striation which has a grained appearance that looks moist and lucid, like glass, and resembles that of polished wood. This type of chinaware is known as *hard paste* porcelain. It is brilliantly white, cold to the touch, impervious to liquids and even to scratching.

## Oriental Export (Chinaware)

Hard paste porcelain was made in China and Japan. In China, the making of porcelain centered in the community of Chingtechen where, by the thirteenth century, the entire population was engaged in some way in the porcelain-making process. The Japanese began to make porcelain about 1500. It is called Imari, after the port from which most of the products were shipped. The body of Japanese porcelain is inferior in quality to that of Chinese, but the decoration is much richer and more diverse.

Although not unknown in the courts of Europe, Oriental Export Chinaware was introduced by the great trading companies in Europe during the eighteenth century. It was greatly admired and highly prized. The name *porcelain* was given to it in Europe because of the resemblance of the finish to a lovely, colorful, glossy tropical marine shell found in the Mediterranean area.

The term *Oriental Export Porcelain* is used to describe all pieces *made* and *decorated* in the Orient more or less according to Western specifications and for Western use, that is, for export only. The trade in this material was developed into a significant phase of international commerce during the eighteenth century, carried on principally between China and Europe. Prior to the American Revolution, English trade laws, for tax purposes, prohibited the importing of any Oriental commodities — even tea — except through England. The direct importing of chinaware into the United States began in 1784, and was never extensive.

Chinaware exported from the Orient falls into two general classes: The ordinary varieties, which were either left undecorated or painted in underglazed colors of which blue-and-white was most popular; and porcelain made to special order. The latter includes armorial porcelain with decorations painted over the glaze, such as the 302-piece table service, with the arms of the Society of Cincinnati, purchased by George Washington in 1786 for use at Mount Vernon (Martha Washington's "company china"). The latter also includes porcelain with "personalized" coats-of-arms or other family identification.

Oriental Export chinaware, unlike most porcelains, has no factory or other marks on the back. Any piece of so-called Oriental Export which has a mark, especially a square pseudo-Chinese mark in red with a running "S" beside it, was made in France. It is an imitation known as Samson, the name of the French manufacturer, who also imitated Meissen, Chelsea, and Bow chinaware.

All Oriental Export chinaware is 150 or more years old. For this reason, minor hairline cracks, small nicks, or minor repairs are to be expected. Elinor Gordon, an American collector, says, "Many collectors are willing to overlook small nicks, chips, or age cracks. It would be foolish to miss the opportunity of acquiring a rare piece because it is imperfect." Such opinions have inspired the creation of miracle-mending materials for the collector as well as the novice.

## Continental European Chinaware

Craftsmen in Europe, examining the imported chinaware, believed it was some kind of glass, and began experiments to reproduce it. They mixed ground glass, lime, soapstone, potash, and sometimes bone-ash, with white clay and other materials to produce a type of china that is known as *soft paste*. This china lacks the cold, brilliant perfection of "true" porcelain; but when glazed with oxide of lead or tin, has a beautiful finish. Like hard paste porcelain, soft paste porcelain is made of earth clays; but the soft paste china is first fired in "biscuit" or bisque stage, that is, unglazed. After the initial firing, decorating is done and a glaze of lead applied before a second firing at lower temperature. Soft paste porcelain is not nearly as resistant as hard paste to liquids or stain, and articles can be easily scratched with a nail file or knife. When broken, the break shows a grainy or sugary surface. The lead coating appears to "sit" on the surface rather than becoming a part of the article. This gives a depth and richness to the decoration, which seems to glow through as though illuminated from behind. No re-firing is necessary in mending, repairing, or restoring.

## Meissen and Dresden Chinaware

Nowhere in Europe was Oriental Export china more popular than in Germany. The rage for this porcelain and for other forms of Oriental art reached its height in the Japanese palace in Dresden, which was never completed. The palace was planned by Augustus the Strong, Elector of Saxony and King of Poland, who wanted every room decorated exclusively with porcelain of which he had thousands of pieces.

Augustus ordered a young alchemist, Johann Friedrich Bottger, to turn his talents from a search for gold by transmutation to a search for the secret of manufacturing porcelain. With the aid of a physicist and mathematician, Tschirnhausen, Bottger was able to do this in 1706, and by 1710, he had established a factory at Meissen, a suburb of Dresden. Augustus had not only the very first hard paste porcelain made in Europe (and as much of it as he wanted since he owned the factory), but all his Chinese pieces as well. Meissen, from 1710 throughout most of the eighteenth century, was produced and decorated by the leading painters of Europe and represents some of the most beautiful and treasured porcelain extant in the world.

This porcelain was known for many years by the name of the Saxon capital, Dresden; however, many other factories sprang up to make commercial china, and the term "Meissen" is now used to identify the old, royal porcelain, while "Dresden" is used for both old and modern china made in other factories. The china menders were not far behind nor long in developing techniques to restore broken treasures.

The difference between Oriental Export porcelain, or China-Trade porcelain, and that made at the royal factory at Meissen and later in other European countries, lies in the forms and decorations used. All are hard paste porcelain, made from the same types of clay.

## English Chinaware

Beginning in the early 1740s, factories for making soft paste chinaware were started in England at Bow and Chelsea and Bristol, Derby, and Worcester; however, no hard paste porcelain was made until about 1768, when a Quaker named Cookworthy discovered deposits of kaolin and petuntse near Plymouth, and took out the first patent for making hard paste chinaware. Thereafter, with the formulas for both soft paste porcelain and hard paste porcelain generally available, the various manufacturers produced whatever the market demanded.

Between the years 1790 and 1810, there came into existence in England a hybrid that was to be known as English bone china. The most prominent name in connection with its development is Josiah Spode, father and son.

The Spode formula was roughly 4 parts of china stone (petuntse) to 3½ parts of china clay (kaolin), with the addition of 6 parts of bone ash, a powdery white calcium phosphate ash produced by burning animal bones. When these three components are fired, the result is a hard paste porcelain softened by the addition of the bone ash. It wears better and is harder and less permeable than soft paste porcelain, but has the same soft type of glaze. It is whiter than soft paste porcelain, but less white and brilliant than hard paste porcelain. Because the new type of china, which has come to be known as English bone china, had the desirable qualities of both hard and soft paste porcelain and could be made considerably more economically, it became generally popular. Today, most of the good quality table services produced in England and the United States are bone china.

# PART II

# CHAPTER SEVEN:
# INSTANT MENDING
# OF CHINAWARE:
# STEP-BY-STEP

# NOTES ABOUT CHINAWARE

Instant mending materials, properly used, enable you to mend many damaged or broken articles made of china. The mending materials, as you have learned, are complex chemical compounds of the laboratory. Chinaware is made in and comes from the Orient, Continental Europe and England, and America.

Chinaware is made from a combination of earth substances, with which the mending materials have been designed to have a special affinity, that is, a special bonding capability. The understanding by the mender of this fact, with the use of the proper materials to mend each type of broken chinaware, makes the miracle of perfect mending come true.

China, which is the product to be covered in this chapter, is the name given to a wide variety of articles that may be referred to elsewhere herein as Oriental Export, Continental European, English, and American. Chinaware may be useful and beautiful, commonplace and rare, easily replaced or duplicated, or treasures lost forever to collectors and museums, if not valued enough to preserve, mend, repair, or restore.

# Damage # 1

*Fill in chipped area using your finger or a brush.*

*Mended pitcher.*

# DAMAGE # 1: A SURFACE FLAKE DAMAGE TO THE GLAZE; BASE OF CHINA PITCHER

The instant mending material to use is Kay-O-Lin. This material meets the need in mending for an acceptable substitute for porcelain. When the two part resin and hardener system is compounded and worked together in equal parts with your fingers, it simulates porcelain effectively. When you have properly filled in the flake chip according to the step-by-step sequence given below, and smoothed it to perfectly match the surface of the pitcher, the material will start to harden and set up in about 45 minutes. The mending operation will take you about 5 minutes.

1. Wash, clean and bleach your pitcher if necessary to get all dirt out of cracks and crevices.

2. Air dry.

3. Prepare equal parts of the Kay-O-Lin resin and hardener, and make a firm compound. Color the clay to match your pitcher, (you may use artist's oil paints, such as Grumbacher's, right out of the tube) as required.

4. Fill in chipped out area using your finger or an art brush.

5. Permit material to get semi-hard, which it will do in about 20 minutes.

6. Dampen fingers in water before material has set, and smooth away excess. Reduces need for sanding, and eliminates the scratching of surrounding areas of glaze.

7. If color matches surrounding area perfectly, apply final coat of New Gloss Glaze. This can be smoothed on with your finger or with an art brush, and brought into perfect harmony with surrounding glazed area.

# Damage # 2

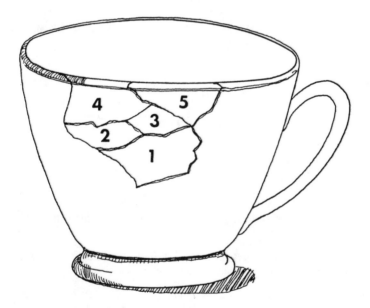

*Cementing into place the broken out pieces of a small bowl or cup requires the sequencing shown above. Install each piece and secure with a bit of Scotch Tape. Number the pieces and tape into place. Once numbered in place, the tape is easily stripped off and the pieces reinstalled and cemented.*

*Retape each piece firmly in place to hold the pieces securely until the cement has had time to harden and dry. Remove the tape when the cement has hardened. Mending time: about 10 minutes. Since this is instant mending, you will not have an invisible mend.*

# DAMAGE # 2: INSTANT MENDING, BROKEN OUT PIECES; CHINA CUP

1. Be sure you have all your pieces.

2. Pierce top of Krazy Glue with plunger-pin and squeeze out enough to treat the edges of adjoining pieces.

3. Press parts together for 10 seconds; permanent mending strength will be achieved almost immediately.

4. When all pieces have been cemented together cement into place in the cup.

5. Secure with masking tape, if necessary, to give full support.

6. Balance in sandbox, and let set.

7. Scrape off excess by dipping razor blade (single edge) into your lacquer thinner. Mending time, less than five minutes, unless you want to paint to match surrounding surface, and then glaze to finish invisibilizing the mend.

## Alternate Step-by-Step Sequence Using DEPEND II

1. Remove syringe (A) tip and depress plunger to apply a small amount of Part (A) to one surface. Pull back slightly on plunger to stop flow. Replace tip.

2. Remove syringe (B) tip and depress plunger to apply a small amount of Part (B) to other surface. Replace tip.

3. Press parts together for 30-45 seconds; permanent mending strength will be achieved in 45 minutes. Again, your actual mending time will be about 5 minutes.

4. Balance article in sandbox, and let set.

5. Scrape off excess by dipping razor blade into your lacquer thinner.

## Damage # 3

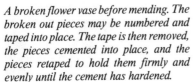

*A broken flower vase before mending. The broken out pieces may be numbered and taped into place. The tape is then removed, the pieces cemented into place, and the pieces retaped to hold them firmly and evenly until the cement has hardened.*

*A flower vase after mending. Excess cement must be removed; then the inside of the vase is reporcelainized and permitted to dry. Redecorating the outside can be accomplished by tracing off the design, taping carbon paper under the tracing paper, and transferring the missing design back onto the surface of the vase. The design can then be followed by using matching oil colors with a bit of Glaze.*

# DAMAGE # 3: AN ARTICLE BROKEN IN PIECES; SUCH AS A PORCELAIN VASE

You may want to use E Pox E Glue for a quick mend. E Pox E Glue provides an extra strong bond. It is transparent and waterproof. Be sure you have washed and dried all surfaces of your vase, so that it is clean, dry, and free of all dust and dirt or smudge spots.

1. Inspect damage to the broken vase for additional hairline cracks and or chips.

2. Plan assembly of the broken pieces.

3. Since this material works in a matter of seconds you will want to assemble any assisting materials needed to do the job. Prepare strips of masking tape in lengths needed to secure the pieces to be fitted into the article.

4. Pierce the seal in the head of each tube and squeeze out equal amounts of each on a clean saucer.

5. Mix thoroughly until you get a uniform clarity to your mending material. This takes a matter of seconds.

6. Apply to each of the surfaces being repaired.

7. Tape each piece together and secure with masking tape.

8. Mending time will take but a few minutes, but the set time for this product is about one hour. It would be best to allow the bond to cure overnight before doing additional work on it.

9. Using a single edge razor blade dipped in acetone or lacquer thinner, clean up excess E Pox E Glue.

10. If you have chips, you should use Kay-O-Lin resin and hardener mixed in equal parts to make a paste. Fill in missing parts or chips with the clay and let harden.

If you are an artist or artistic and want to invisibilize your mend, you will want to use Grumbacher Oil Paints to color your Kay-O-Lin clay to match existing surfaces; also to paint in prior existing design. When finished, you will want to use New Gloss Glaze to blend in your work with existing surfaces.

**HOW TO MEND A
PORCELAIN VASE
AND RESTORE THE
DESIGN**

*The vase shown was broken in three fairly even pieces. However, had
there been more pieces, these would first be numbered and installed by
using Scotch Tape to secure each piece in place. Once numbered,
remove tapes from these pieces and cement in place.*

*The problem is to conceal the outside cracks which disfigure the vase.
This is done by using tracing paper to trace off segments of the floral
design. Then use Scotch Tape to secure carbon paper to the underside
of the tracing paper and retrace the design on the vase, using a sharp,
hard lead pencil. The design will transfer to the porcelain and needs
only to be painted on. Mix the colors used with a touch of New Gloss
Glaze for finish and hardener.*

# DAMAGE # 4: MENDING A BROKEN PLATE; CHINAWARE

1. Clean and dry all residue, dirt or soil from the broken pieces.

2. Pierce tip of container and apply a thin coat of the ADHESIVE to each edge, joining them together as you work.

3. Secure in place with masking tape, as you go.

4. Fit pieces firmly together and squeeze out excess material to allow assembly of all pieces evenly, with edges fitted perfectly. Support pieces whenever and as necessary with masking tape.

5. Remove excess ADHESIVE as soon as possible by wiping with a piece of cheesecloth or a paper napkin. After ADHESIVE is completely cured, excess material can be removed by trimming with a sharp blade. Avoid under cutting your seal.

6. After use, replace tube cap and tighten securely.

A broken-out edge chip or lip chip is a damage that may occur when one or more pieces are broken. The broken out V in the side or lip edge may be mended by using Kay-O-lin clay mix with a backup support of masking tape.

1. Prepare the Kay-O-lin resin and hardener mix in equal parts and make a fairly firm paste. Color to match existing broken pieces.

2. Press into place, support with masking tape.

3. Smooth off excess by dipping your finger into water or acetone. Make sure edges match existing surfaces perfectly. Reduces need for sanding.

4. Balance in sandbox. Allow to cure.

5. If edging is gold leaf, you may buy a small vial of gold bronze powder. Apply by mixing a small quantity with your nail polish. Feather-out gently with your finger until matching edges join invisibly.

*HOW TO RESTORE A PLATE USING INSTANT MENDING MATERI-ALS: The several breaks may involve broken edges with large chips or flake chips.*

*Let us try Adhesive. Apply to each of the surfaces of the pieces to be joined together. Normally, Adhesive cures in 5 minutes, fully cures and bonds in 24 hours.*

*Mended plate.*

# DAMAGE # 5: A CUP WITH A BROKEN HANDLE; CHINAWARE

1. Use Krazy Glue, or Super Glue or Permabond. Any of these three materials will bond in seconds. You will have to have some solvent handy, such as acetone to prevent any escaping drop from bonding your fingers together.

2. Carefully pierce end of tube with pin. Only one drop applied to each surface.

3. Firmly press each piece together for 30-45 seconds. An instant bond will take place; once all the pieces have been cemented together.

4. Apply cement to the top and bottom ends. Set aside.

5. Apply cement to the nubs.

6. Apply handle to the nubs in a perfect match so that the fit is even. Hold cup and handle firmly in your grasp for 30-45 seconds.

7. Balance in sand box and allow to set. The bonding and the cure are almost instantaneous. Mending time: about five minutes altogether.

However, you will want to be sure your cup will hold liquid, hot or cold, and be serviceable. You can assure yourself of this by taking a few extra mending steps.

## Securing a Handle to a Cup with Additional Mending Material Called Kay-O-Lin

1. Mix this resin and hardener in equal parts.

2. Color to match your cup, using Grumbacher Oil paints.

3. Keep your hands immaculately clean. Use your lacquer thinner or acetone and paper napkins. Moisten your Kay-O-lin paste or putty clay and apply smoothly and evenly to cover the mended handle. Also, apply putty around the ends joined to the cup nubs. This will take about 5 more minutes. Set cup aside in sand box and allow 24 hours for complete cure. Actually, the clay will set up in about 45 minutes, but it is better to be on the safe side and permit it to harden into stone. Since you have colored to match your cup, the handle need only be glazed with New Gloss Glaze to complete restoration.

*For a cup with a handle broken in two pieces (left), mending must rejoin the handle to a section that is also broken out of the cup. The nub left on the back of the cup (far right) forms a base on which to mold or rebuild the handle.*

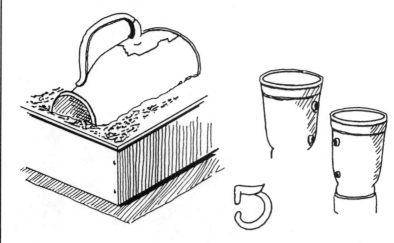

# Damage # 6

*Cup mended following steps as illustrated on pages 58–61.*

# DAMAGE # 6: CUP WITH BROKEN HANDLE ATTACHED TO BROKEN OUT PIECE

1. Use Krazy Glue, or Super Glue or Permabond. Any of these three materials will bond in seconds. You will have to have some solvent handy, such as acetone to prevent any escaping drop from bonding your fingers together.

2. Carefully pierce end of tube with pin. Only one drop applied to each surface.

3. Firmly press each broken piece together and hold for 30-45 seconds. An instant bond will take place; once all the pieces have been cemented together.

4. Apply cement to rough edges of cup where the broken out piece fits.

5. Apply cement to the bottom nub of the cup.

6. Apply handle and broken out piece into opening where the fit must be made perfect. Be sure the bottom nub is securely anchored to the bottom end of the handle.

7. Use masking tape to fasten securely in place and allow a set time of 5 minutes.

Because the broken out piece constitutes a severe and weakening damage to the body of the cup, you will want to be sure your cup is restored to serviceable use. You can assure yourself of this by taking a few extra steps described on pages 60–61.

*3. Firmly press pieces together.*

*4. Apply cement to rough edges of cup.*

5. *Apply cement to the bottom nub of the cup.*

6. *Apply handle and broken out piece.*

## Secure the Mending You Have Done
## With Additional Mending Material
## Called Kay-O-Lin

1. Mix this resin and hardener in equal parts.

2. Color to match your cup using Grumbacher Oil paints.

3. Clean your hands and fingers. Wipe off any mending material with Acetone or lacquer thinner. Dry your hands with paper napkins. These materials will not adversely affect even the most sensitive skin, as they are commonly used with nail polish.

4. Moisten your Kay-O-lin putty clay and apply smoothly and evenly to cover the mended lines. Apply putty to the two broken cracks on the rim of the cup and smooth the putty down over the lip so that it is applied inside the cup as well as on the outside.

5. Now apply the putty clay around the end joined to the nub on the cup. This will take about 5 minutes more mending time, but it is as well worth the effort as it will help invisibilize the mend as well as guarantee a firm mending job and serviceability of your cup.

6. Set cup aside in sand box and allow 24 hours for a complete cure. Actually, the clay will set up in about 45 minutes, but it is better to be on the safe side and permit the material to harden into stone. Since you have colored the material to match your cup, the handle need only be glazed with New Gloss Glaze to complete the restoration. Entire mending time — 10 minutes.

You may find that all surfaces are not perfectly blended with the rest of the cup, but bear in mind, you have elected to use instant mending materials rather than go to a school to learn professional mending techniques.

Whenever you use an instant bonding material the excess must be cleaned off or wiped off by using a bit of cheese cloth or a paper napkin dipped into lacquer thinner or acetone. The bond as well as a few extra minutes must be allowed for the curing time before using lacquer thinner or acetone to wipe away the excess material or it may all fall apart. However, once the bond and cure have taken place the solvent will not affect the mend. Carefully clean away any excess using both the solvent and a razor blade to apply the colored matching Kay-O-lin putty. You may apply the putty paste with an artist brush or by using your finger, frequently dipping brush or finger into the solvent to effect an even smooth spread of the material. Remember to apply this mix until all edges and surfaces are perfectly blended and none of the mended lines are showing, both on the inside as well as on the outside of the mends. This mix will harden into a porcelain like substance that should match or very closely match your broken article. It will be unaffected after curing by washing. After glazing, apply art gold decoration, if required.

*Securing the mending.*

# Damage # 7

*Apply bonding.*

*Set aside in sand box and allow curing time of several minutes.*

# DAMAGE # 7: A BROKEN BASE OR PEDESTAL ON A COMPOTE; CHINAWARE

1. Inspect damage to the broken base for additional chips, cracks, or missing pieces.

2. The top part or bowl of the compote is the heavier of the two pieces, if only the base is broken off. If the top is broken in several pieces, you will have to mend that first. And the same with the base. When you have the broken article reduced to top and bottom, you will have a balancing problem because of the weight of the top bowl. So reverse the bowl part and balance the base on the protruding stem just to get the feel of the problem, and to determine the exact fit. Prepare to mend this difficult article with instant mending or bonding material such as Krazy Glue, Super Glue, or Permabond. Have your masking tape ready so that after you have bonded the two pieces together, you can apply tape around the mend to provide for additional support. Ready?

3. Now that you are thoroughly prepared to tackle this difficult mend, plan assembly of the broken pieces.

4. Prepare strips of masking tape in lengths needed to secure the pieces to be fitted into the article.

5. Apply instant bonding material to the broken pieces of the bowl, closely or perfectly fitting their edges together. Always glue your broken pieces together first. Then apply them as one piece to the broken article.

6. Fit the assembled pieces into the bowl and apply your instant bonding material. You may prefer to apply your bonding material to the broken edges first, but either way, be sure you have achieved a perfect fit.

7. Wipe off excess with a paper napkin or paper towel dipped in lacquer thinner. Allow surface to dry.

8. Clean off any excess still remaining with a razor blade dipped into the solvent.

9. Follow above procedures in mending the base.

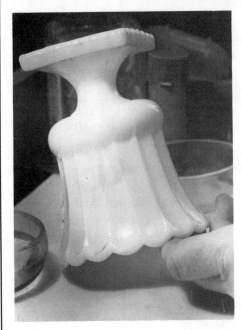

*Turn bowl upside down and apply bonding material.*

*Mended bowl.*

10. Turn your bowl upside down and apply bonding material to the broken end of the stem or nub. Apply material to the broken end of the stem on the base. Now fit and balance the two pieces and hold them securely for a space of about a minute to make sure of their bond. Apply masking tape to secure mend.

11. Set aside in sandbox and allow curing time of several minutes.

12. Remove masking tape.

13. Using a razor blade dipped in lacquer thinner or acetone, remove all excess bonding glue. Clean surface thoroughly. Wipe with paper towel or napkin dipped in thinner.

The following steps are optional and suggested in the event you want to invisibilize your mend.

1. Prepare a mix of equal parts of Kay-O-lin putty clay.

2. Use Grumbacher's Oil paint or zinc to color the putty clay to match your broken article.

3. Moisten the clay with thinner to a paste-like consistency. Apply over breaks and mends with an art brush or with your moistened finger until the clay is smoothed and blended with surrounding surfaces.

4. Allow clay to dry (about 45 minutes).

5. Brush on New Gloss Glaze for finish.

6. If you are mending a decorated article and feel you have the time and talent, paint in the decoration using Grumbacher's Oil paints. Permit 24 hours for set.

7. Reglaze, for final finish.

# Damage # 8

*A broken soup tureen before repair, with multiple breaks and chips, and the top ornamental finial broken off.*

# DAMAGE # 8: A BROKEN LID: PORCELAIN

You may have a broken soup tureen lid, with multiple breaks and chips, and the top ornamental finial may also be broken off.

1. Inspect damaged pieces of broken lid to see how you can fit them together. If you have but a single break or just the finial broken off, you may want to use Krazy Glue, Super Glue, or Permabond. Any one of the three will do an instant mending job for you. If you have multiple breaks, any of these materials may be used to reunite the broken article and you will want to use Kay-O-lin putty clay colored to match existing surfaces, to fill in the chips or missing pieces.

2. Plan assembly of the broken pieces.

3. Prepare strips of masking tape in lengths needed to secure the pieces to be fitted together and into the broken lid.

4. Pierce the tip of the instant bonding material tube and apply the liquid sparingly to each of the edges of the broken pieces, as you fit them together.

5. When you have assembled all the broken pieces and fitted them together, cement the piece into place and secure with masking tape from both the inside and the outside.

## Chips and Invisibilizing

1. Prepare equal parts of Kay-O-lin putty-clay. Mix well with your fingers until you have a firm ball of material.

2. Color your putty clay with Grumbacher Oil paints and moisten as you go, with lacquer thinner or acetone. Your putty clay must match the lid on which you are working as you will not want the chips to show.

3. Fill in each and every chip and smooth until the clay is perfectly even with surrounding surfaces.

4. Set aside to dry and harden. Mending time: about 15 minutes. Curing time for putty clay: 45 minutes. Better to let stand overnight or 24 hours.

# Damage # 8

*Plan assembly of broken pieces.*

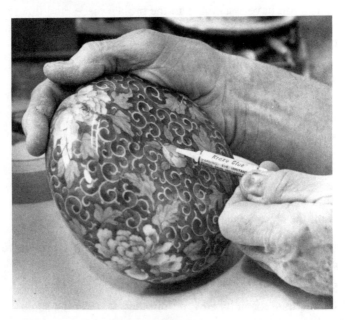

*Apply instant bonding material sparingly.*

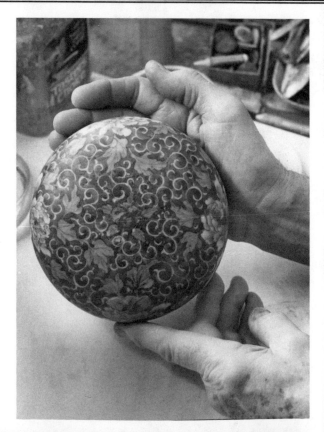

*Mended lid.*

# Damage # 9

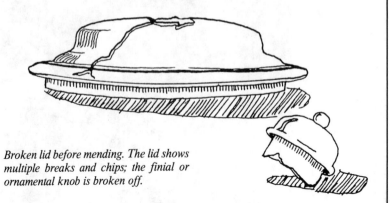

*Broken lid before mending. The lid shows multiple breaks and chips; the finial or ornamental knob is broken off.*

*Lid after mending following the steps on page 71.*

# DAMAGE # 9: A FINIAL BROKEN OFF A LID; PORCELAIN OR CHINAWARE

1. If the finial is missing, you may be able to mold a finial by hand.

2. Prepare Kay-O-Lin resin and hardener putty clay in equal parts and mix into a firm ball, rolled in your hand. Add a proper base to fit the place where the finial is missing. Color with Grumbacher Oil Paints.

3. If the hole goes clear through the lid, prepare lengths of masking tape and apply to the underside of the lid to cover the hole. Be sure clay matches.

4. Blend and firmly press clay mix into the hole and surrounding edges, until the base you are preparing will take a stem or upright piece of clay as a proper support for the clay ball, which is to serve as a finial. Allow set time of 45 minutes.

5. Prepare the stem support for the finial. Shape and blend into the base. Between each procedure with the clay, you must allow at least 45 minutes setting time, so that you can be assured of a firm structure. Permit stem to set.

6. Apply the ball of clay or finial. You may have given this top piece a bit of shaping such as shown in the illustration. After application, permit finial to set overnight.

7. Remove excess cement. If edges are showing, mix additional quantity of putty-clay, colored to match existing and blend in over all exposed edge. Apply evenly all around the mend, using your fingers dipped in acetone or lacquer thinner.

8. Remove excess. This is extremely important as Kay-O-Lin will harden into a stone-like substance, and once married to the article it is irremovable without damage to the appearance of the mend.

9. Apply New Gloss Glaze to finish coating the mend.

# Damage # 10

*HOW TO MEND A COFFEE-POT SPOUT: Use Kay-O-lin putty-clay. Mix the Resin and Hardener 50/50 in sufficient quantity to build, shape, and smooth the mend to blend with surrounding surfaces. The putty must be colored to match existing surrounding surfaces.*

*If the entire spout is broken into many pieces, you will have to glue them together first and fit them to the coffeepot with an instant bonding material, such as Krazy Glue.*

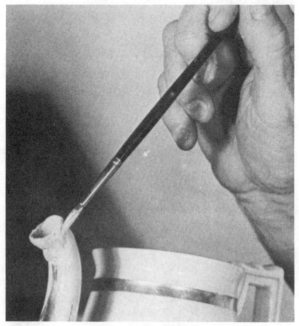

*After applying the putty mix, blend and smooth with an art brush.*

# DAMAGE # 10: A BROKEN COFFEEPOT SPOUT; CHINA

1. Use Kay-O-lin putty-clay in equal parts. Mix thoroughly to make a firm paste of the putty resin and hardener. Make a sufficient quantity to build, shape, and smooth-coat the mend.

2. Prepare strips of masking tape in lengths needed to provide a firm support and base to hold your clay mix in place. Color your clay mix to match your article.

3. You are now ready to use the cementing putty mix to model the spout carefully. Shape it as it was, and give it a slight trough in the middle to provide good pouring.

4. Keep smoothing and shaping the cement mix with your fingers or with an art brush dipped in lacquer thinner. Be careful to use the thinner sparingly so that your putty clay cement mix remains firm.

Mending time about 10 minutes. Curing time about 45 minutes. However, it is best to allow the putty clay to set overnight or for 24 hours for a complete cure. The clay will harden into a porcelain-like stone.

5. Apply New Gloss Glaze.

6. If the spout rim was edged in gold, use an art brush to apply a gold edging with Gold Bronze powder, or you may use an art gold in paste form. Apply carefully, as directed on the package.

*A coffeepot with a piece of the edging broken out of the spout.*

# Damage # 11

*A chinaware article that has been cracked or fractured requires careful examination before it is boiled. First, examine the edges. Are the edges of the crack tight together, or can you insert a razor blade between them? Is the crack dirty, or are the edges aged and yellowed or discolored? Whether the edges are tight together or loose, boil out any possible discoloration and dirt. Use an enamel pan or bucket big-enough and deep-enough to enable you to submerge the article. The cracked part must be completely covered. After the crack is truly clean and seems to have disappeared, air dry it, and treat the crack as outlined on the following page.*

# DAMAGE # 11: CRACKS AND FRACTURES; CHINA PLATE

1. Determine whether the crack is tight or loose, that is, whether the edges can be spread apart or are immovable. If the edges of the crack(s) can be spread apart with a bit of pressure, the plate cannot be mended with instant mending techniques. If the hairlines or fractures are immovable, proceed as follows:

2. Boil article, completely immersing the dish in water.

3. After boiling remove and immediately place the dish or article in a waiting container filled with pure bleach such as Clorox. (See page 76.)

4. Allow the article to remain in this bleach until no cracks or hairlines can be seen. Inspect closely. This may take a few minutes, or as much as three days.

5. When you are satisfied that no lines can be seen, remove article, wash thoroughly in soapy water and dry.

6. Apply New Gloss Glaze to seal. (See page 77.)

Above process takes only a few minutes of your time, but is an interrupted process, and the only one known to the author to eliminate craze-ing, hairlines or cracks that cannot be spread. The process for removing large spread apart cracks that are badly discolored and or full of dirt is given in the professional mending section of this book.

*Place plate in a plastic pan. Pour pure bleach over the plate until it is covered. Let the plate soak until the cracks disappear.*

*Remove the plate from the plastic pan; wash and dry thoroughly.*

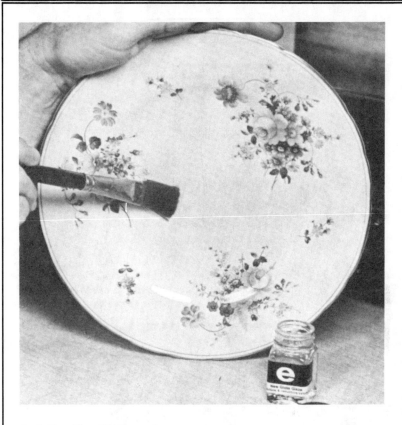

*Apply New Gloss Glaze to seal.*

# Damage # 12

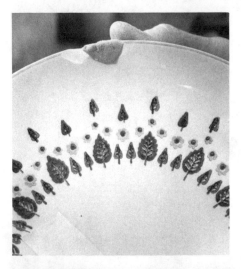

*The Kay-O-lin putty clay can be worked into a flake chip, lip or edge chip, or can be substituted for a small missing part.*

*After curing, the article may be touched up with oil paints and New Gloss Glaze.*

# DAMAGE # 12: MISSING PARTS OF CHINAWARE, PORCELAIN AND POTTERY

The process of restoring missing parts is described elsewhere in the book.

However, it is again mentioned here, as very minor parts may be missing such as a flaked out lip chip on the base of a cup handle may be missing and not the entire handle. Or a handle off a vegetable dish or soup tureen or casserole. A missing finial may be cleverly restored by a person with a thumb that is happy to serve like a sculptor's thumb and push, mold, and shape the nicest finial you ever saw.

Many people are amazingly talented and do not realize it until they meet the challenge and suddenly discover their ability.

A solidly shaped handle missing from a vegetable dish or soup tureen can be shaped out of the instant mending material known as Kay-O-lin and applied to the dish with supporting masking tape to hold it in place.

1. Classify the damage (flake chip, lip or edge chip, missing part, missing piece, missing solid handle).

2. Use a 50/50 mix of Kay-O-lin resin and hardener.

3. Color to match your article with Grumbacher Oil paints. If white, use Grumbacher's Zinc. Avoid Acrylic paints.

4. The Kay-O-lin putty clay, when colored to match the area surrounding the damage, can be worked into a flake chip, lip or edge chip, or can be substituted to fill in a small missing part. The hand molding process should take only a few minutes.

5. Smooth and blend your material with your moistened fingers to avoid having to sand the material later. If you have a good color match, the blended material should join to the edges smoothly. It is well to smooth the putty clay out over the edges a fraction of an inch, overlapping them so that the mend will be less obvious.

6. Set aside the article, balance in sandbox if necessary, and allow the material to cure for 24 hours.

# CHAPTER EIGHT:
# INSTANT MENDING OF GLASSWARE:
# STEP-BY-STEP

# NOTES ABOUT GLASSWARE

Glass is a substance composed chiefly of silica, which is obtained from a vitreous sand of the right grain and free from impurities. Other components are calcium oxide and several alkaline fluxes. Calcium oxide makes the glass resistant and constant, and enhances its brilliance. Alkaline fluxes such as sodium oxide and potassium oxide enable the glass to be melted and manipulated. These fluxes, with the addition of lime and sometimes lead oxide, give to glass an amorphous character — glass is not crystalline in structure, unlike rock crystal which it otherwise resembles closely.

Glass is made by fusing its components at high temperature into a fiery, molten liquid. This liquid is used in two principal ways to form objects of glassware: molding and blowing. Molding is by far the older process. A mold in the form of the exterior of the article to be made is first constructed, the interior being formed by a core. The molten glass is then carefully poured into the mold and allowed to cool.

As an intermediate step between molding and blowing, liquid glass was blown through a tube into prepared molds. A modern refinement of this ancient process is employed today in the mass production of glass bottles.

Glassblowing is a technique requiring a high degree of skill. Glass in a thickening liquid state can be "gathered" on the end of a long, hollow tube and, by man's breath, blown into a round bubble. This is the first step in making an article of blown glassware. As the bubble is reheated and swung at the end of the blowpipe, a cylinder is formed. At the precise state of soft, pliable firmness, the cylinder is transferred from the end of the blowpipe to a pontil (rod). Thereafter, it is maintained in this condition to be cut with shears and manipulated into the required shape.

All articles of glassware were made by these two processes until the invention in the latter part of the 17th century of a way to make flat or plate glass for commercial purposes.

# Damage # 1

*Wineglass with a missing piece.*

*Coat with New Gloss Glaze for an almost invisible mend.*

# DAMAGE # 1: BROKEN OUT EDGE CHIP OR LIP CHIP, THREE CORNER DAMAGE

Note illustration. The glass shown with the three corner damage illustrates a glass with a missing piece.

1. Secure Scotch tape to each side, top, and bottom to form a channel or "footer" into which you can drip the Crystal Clear material, drop by drop, until the channel has been filled. Never mind unevenness, because this excess material will not cure and can be wiped away later, after curing of the rest of the material.

2. Set the glass in sunlight.

3. Allow time for the material to cure 10-20 seconds. This is a quick-drying, quick-curing material and only the material in the channel will cure, not the material which is excess to the mend. (Mystery, even the manufacturer of the material cannot tell why only the mending material cures and leaves the rest as excess, that is the way it works.)

4. When cured, remove the glass from the sunlight. Gently and carefully remove the walls of Scotch tape. Wipe off excess material using a paper napkin. Wash the glass in warm, clear, sudsy water.

5. Permit the glass to stand and dry.

6. Apply a light coat of New Gloss Glaze over the mend to blend mended edges in with the surrounding surfaces of the glass, as necessary.

7. Dry in sunlight.

# DAMAGE # 2: BROKEN STEM OF WINE GLASS; GLASSWARE

To repair a broken stem of a wine glass, you will need your sand-box, as you will have a balancing problem, which can only be overcome by inversion of the glass, held at just the right angle by the sand. You will need both working hands to do the mending job.

1. Classify damage. Is it a clean break? Has the break occurred half way up the stem or at the very base? Do you have a shattered stem? If the stem is shattered and you have all the pieces these pieces must first be assembled and fitted together using Krazy Glue or Super Glue and Perma Bond. You will need an instant bonding material. Use this material sparingly, a drop at a time, until your pieces are fitted together and ready to be rejoined to the stem. Another problem. If the stem is broken at an angle, you will have to lay the glass on its side in the sand and gently join the assembled pieces, base, and stem. Instant bonding is your only hope of success. If the problem is beyond instant mending, refer to the professional section of this book dealing with exactly this problem.

2. Once you are ready to join your stem pieces together, you may find it helpful to apply Scotch tape to the underside of the pieces to be joined.

3. Fit the pieces together leaving the ends of the Scotch tape open.

4. Apply instant bonding material.

5. Close tape ends.

6. Bonding is almost instantaneous, however, it would be well to allow curing time or hardening time of several minutes.

7. Use a single edge razor blade, dipped in acetone or lacquer thinner and remove Scotch tape supports.

8. Clean away all excess material with razor blade.

9. Glaze stem with New Gloss Glaze, to help invisibilize the mend.

# DAMAGE # 3 and 4: EDGE, LIP, AND FLAKE CHIPS ON GLASSES, ETC.

**Note:** Glass is not repairable with glass. Nor can a missing part be reblown and added. Glass has a melting temperature of above 1200 degrees. That is when glass blowers work with glass. Obviously, glass that is white hot at 1200 degrees cannot be applied to cold glass, as it would shatter it into a thousand fragments.

Glass may be soft or hard. If soft, it is made with lime. If hard, it may be made with lead and silver, making a dazzling fine crystal.

Glass may be thin or thick. If it is thin, you may be able to eliminate edge chips by using great care and a diamond file. If thick, you may be able to fill in the edge chips with Crystal Clear or Liquid Lucite (obtainable from the author) and you will have least trouble filing with a diamond file.

1. Examine and classify damage (edge chip depth and number of chips, lip chip, flake chip, etc.). If glass is very thin, use diamond file and gently apply with a rocking motion, while holding the glass under tepid tap water.

2. If the chips are multiple, you may prefer to apply scotch tape to the inside and outside of the glass making a channel into which you may carefully apply Crystal Clear, drop by drop, and fill the chipped out edge until it is once again even with the rest of the rim of the glass.

3. Set in sunlight and allow a few seconds for the Crystal Clear to dry and cure.

4. Remove from sunlight. Strip away scotch tape. Wipe away any excess material with paper napkin. Wash and dry.

5. If glass is thick and the chips are deep, using the diamond file will be of little use. Apply scotch tape to the inside and outside of the glass rim, making a channel and proceed as described in steps 2, 3, and 4.

## Damage 3 & 4

For mending edge chips, such as lip chips, flake chips, etc. use Crystal Clear. Crystal Clear has a crystalline quality and will defer eventual yellowing of material. Working time 5 minutes. Curing time, 10–15 seconds in sunlight.

After mend is finished, do not use acetone or lacquer thinner to clean glass of excess material. Use a paper napkin. Then wash in warm, clear, sudsy water. Excess material will not cure and is easily removed.

*If the chips are multiple, you may prefer to apply scotch tape to the inside and outside of the glass making a channel into which you may carefully apply Crystal Clear.*

## Damage # 5

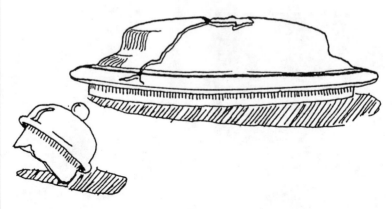

*The broken lid is shown before repair with multiple breaks and chip. The finial or ornamental knob usually fixed to the top is also broken off, and a bad crack shows through the lid.*

*The multiple breaks may mean a few extra minutes, as each chip must be filled individually, the finial cemented back on. As a final operation, the entire lid must be glazed with New Gloss Glaze to seal the crack in the lid.*

# DAMAGE # 5: A FINIAL BROKEN OFF A LID, CHIPPED EDGES, AND A CRACK; GLASSWARE

1. Apply Scotch tape to both the inside and the outside edges of each chipped out place.

2. Use Crystal Clear. Fill chipped out channel drop by drop.

3. Set aside in sunlight to cure, for about 10-20 seconds.

4. Remove Scotch tape supports, and wipe away excess material.

5. Use Krazy Glue. Cover the edges of the lid where the finial fits with spare drops of Crazy Glue. Apply the glue to the finial's broken edges as well.

6. Press the finial firmly into place in exact fitting.

7. Allow a  few minutes curing time, and remove excess material ·with razor blade dipped in acetone or lacquer thinner.

8. Use New Gloss Glaze on the underside of the lid covering the surface in its entirety. Permit drying and curing time of 45 minutes. (Work in a warm, dry area.)

9. Coat the outside with New Gloss Glaze and permit drying and curing time of 45 minutes or more. This will ensure the crack will not leak and will not spread.

## Damage # 6

The drawing of the cup at the left shows a broken handle opposite remaining nubs on the cup. This handle must be mended with instant bonding material such as Krazy Glue, Perma Bond or Super Glue. The repair can be made firm enough to support the cup filled with liquid and the mend can be made almost invisible by using a finishing coat of New Gloss Glaze.

The drawing at the right shows the handle when properly fitted and joined or bonded.

# DAMAGE # 6: MENDING A CUP WITH A BROKEN HANDLE; GLASSWARE

1. Study the article. Assemble the broken shards and fit them together before bonding to make sure they all fit and that you have all the pieces. In the illustration, just two pieces are shown. So your first step, after study and fit, is to apply your instant bonding material to each piece and make a single handle to be joined or rejoined to your glass cup.

2. Allow a few minutes for the bonding material to cure and harden.

3. Remove excess. Scrape the handle clean wherever pieces have been joined. Use a single edge razor blade and dip it in acetone or lacquer thinner to make the cleaning job easy.

4. Apply Super Glue or Krazy Glue to the nubs of the cup and to the top and bottom ends of the handle.

5. Have a few lengths of masking tape ready.

6. Press the handle firmly onto the nubs of the cup. Allow setting time of about 30 seconds. Balance in sandbox, and apply masking tape, attaching the ends of the tape to each side of the cup and securing the handle.

7. Allow the cup to set overnight.

8. Using a razor blade, clean off excess.

9. Apply New Gloss Glaze to entire handle and to the nubs or joints for final finish, and to help invisibilize the mend.

# DAMAGE # 7: PIECE MISSING IN THE BASE OR SIDE OF A VASE; GLASSWARE

1. If the vase is large enough for your hand to be inserted inside, apply Scotch tape or masking tape over the hole from the inside. If you cannot get your hand down into the vase, you do not have an instant mending job, unless you can get a child to paste the tape over the hole from the inside. Covering the hole firmly from the inside is required prior to any following step.

2. Use sufficient quantity of Kay-O-lin clay to make a doughnut around the hole on the outside, to the depth needed to contain the filling material.

3. Place the vase in your sandbox and be sure it is on even keel, absolutely level, side to be mended straight up.

4. Apply Crystal Clear to fill hole.

5. Set entire sandbox containing the vase in the sunlight. Permit several seconds for material to harden and cure. If material seems to have shrunk, add a drop at a time until you have applied several layers, permitting each layer to cure in between applications. Such may not be necessary, as the material used will cure only to the rim. Spillage will not cure, nor will excess material.

6. Permit vase to remain undisturbed for a few minutes.

7. Remove excess material with paper napkin. Do not use acetone or lacquer thinner to remove as it will turn the mended spot into a whitened opaque blemish.

8. Carefully remove the doughnut of Kay-O-lin. Since this clay is also water soluble, you may wash the surface clean, in warm sudsy water.

9. Apply New Gloss Glaze, and allow curing time of 45 minutes.

10. Remove tape from inside vase, and glaze inside with New Gloss Glaze.

# DAMAGE # 8: BROKEN BASE OF AN ARTICLE; GLASS PITCHER

1.  Assemble your pieces and tape them all in place to see if you have a perfect match and all the necessary pieces. If a piece is missing, you will not be able to mend the pitcher with instant mending materials. A piece missing out of the base will require professional techniques and liquid lucite. (A heavy two part resin and hardener that requires 24 hours curing and hardening time.)

2.  Remove tapes and fit all loose pieces together by applying instant bonding material, as you go.

3.  When all loose pieces have been joined, allow the assembly to harden for a few minutes. Clean off excess.

4.  Use a single edge razor blade. Dip edge into acetone or lacquer thinner, cleaning surface of glass and drying with a paper napkin or cheesecloth. Leave no spots or excess on either side.

5.  Apply Krazy Glue or Super Glue or Permabond to all exposed surface edges of the assembled piece. Also to the broken base edges of the pitcher.

6.  Join the base to the pitcher. Permit the mend to cure and harden, a matter of a few minutes.

7.  Again remove any squeezed out material or excess with a paper napkin or cheesecloth. Dip napkin or cloth into your lacquer thinner and clean the mend thoroughly, leaving no trace or spot of the bonding material.

8.  Apply New Gloss Glaze both inside and out to seal the mend permanently and to help invisibilize where it was mended.

# Damage # 8

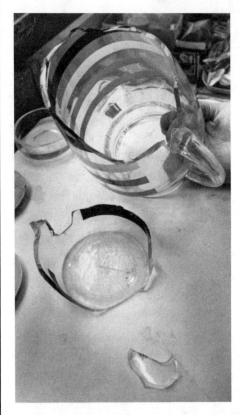

*Assemble pieces.*

*Apply instant bonding as you go.*

*Apply Krazy Glue or Super Glue or Permabond to all exposed edges of the assembled piece.*

*Clean the mend thoroughly.*

# DAMAGE # 9: HAIRLINE CRACK, FRACTURES, A SPREADING CRACK ALMOST ACROSS A GLASS BOWL OR PUNCH BOWL

## Statement of the Problem

A sudden change in room temperature can result in causing a serious damage to your cut glass punch bowl. The bowl is probably deep, with well rounded extended curved sides. These have already been deeply cut. There is tremendous tension in a curve, any curve, even on a highway. Sudden temperature changes can cause your bowl to crack. If you are going to use your bowl for a party, put the punch in first, then the ice cubes. When you wash the bowl, make sure it is room temperature and is no longer icy cold before putting it under hot water. If you put an ice cold bowl under hot water, it will break it in two or severely crack the bowl. It is also almost axiomatic in the mending business to regard something cracked as virtually unmendable. The following "mending" process will not eliminate the crack, but may preserve your bowl and render it serviceable, again.

1. Determine whether the crack is tight or loose, that is, whether the edges can be spread apart or are immovable.

2. If immovable, you are in luck, as you will need only use New Gloss Glaze to coat the inside of the bowl, to preserve it and to keep the crack from spreading.

3. Apply several coats of the glaze between drying time periods.

4. If the crack can be spread a little, but is still "tight" follow the same procedure.

5. If the crack can be spread apart, bind the bowl with masking tape around the outside.

6. Mix the two part system of Liquid Lucite, resin and hardener (obtainable from the author) and carefully apply several coats, allowing overnight drying time between each coat. The Liquid Lucite will set up in about 1 hour. But the curing time will take at least 24 hours. However, it will save your bowl and restore it to future usefulness.

# CHAPTER NINE:
# INSTANT MENDING OF
# POTTERY AND
# STONEWARE:
# STEP-BY-STEP

# NOTES ABOUT POTTERY
# AND STONEWARE

Pottery is a ware shaped from clay. Clay is a fine-grained form of natural material, malleable when wet, that contains primarily hydrated silicates of aluminum. Articles of this material, after being formed, are heat-treated at varying temperatures in their manufacture. The mending materials used on broken or damaged pottery require no firing, although when set and hardened, they become stonelike.

*Two types of pottery:* While there are as many types of decorations on pottery as there have been artisans through the centuries to devise them —from the elaborately enameled and bejeweled pottery of ancient China to the colorful patterns of Pennsylvania-German slipware and sgraffito —there are only two types of pottery the mender needs to know about for mending purposes. These are soft-paste earthenware, which has a high lime content, and hard-paste earthenware containing no lime (see Appendix). In composition and thickness of the body, hard-paste earthenware is often similar to stoneware and porcelain.

## Stoneware

The simplest form of pottery is earthenware, which is merely baked clay. When it is baked at a very high temperature, the clay melts into a solid mass impervious to liquids. This is stoneware. The Chinese, about 100 B.C., made some excellent stoneware that was glazed with a rich yellow and leaf-green.

In Europe, Germany took the lead in the 12th and 13th centuries in making stoneware. It was peculiar to the country, because it was made of pipeclay found chiefly in the Rhineland. The clay was mixed with felspar, quartz, and fireclay, generally used for making firebricks and crucibles, and the articles were given only one firing. Often handfuls of salt were thrown into the kiln at its greatest heat to produce salt-glaze stoneware.

## Soft-paste Pottery

In England particularly, where there was a great demand for table services, most of which were white salt-glaze stoneware, the commercial potters began searching for a cheap but durable substitute that could be more easily manufactured than stoneware.

Josiah Wedgewood, who was well-established in the pottery business, discovered a new material that came to be known as Queens Ware. It looked expensive, was easy to make, was durable but considerably lighter in weight than stoneware, and was comparatively cheap. Under the patronage of Queen Charlotte, this ware became popular, and in a short time, drove salt-glaze stoneware off the market.

# HOW TO USE KAY-O-LIN PUTTY-CLAY WITH OTHER BONDING MATERIALS

Kay-O-lin is a resin and hardener two part system composed of two solid materials, which, when mixed together in equal parts, forms a very strong adhesive bonding material. Because it is a claylike substance, that can be worked in with the fingers, it can be used to fill in cracks, missing pieces, holes, make rough surfaces smooth and it may be used in mending heavy-bodied articles of chinaware as well as for all articles of pottery. When no other material can be used to bond "fire-brick" type pottery because of its porousness, Kay-O-lin will serve very nicely to do the job.

Pottery differs from any other ware in the density of the clay paste with which it is made. And the clay used does not have the purity of Kaolin, which is used to make fine porcelain. Therefore, the materials needed to mend it must be varied to meet the porosity of the pottery article.

Stoneware is a heavy, non-porous pottery made from moist clay hardened by heat. It may be made to look delicate and lovely (Wedgewood being among the most beautiful of such examples of stoneware), but stoneware is indeed heavier, tougher, and harder to break than porcelain.

The durability of pottery and stoneware may be downgraded when you consider how much easier it is to chip than to break. Naturally, pottery and stoneware have more silica in the making and bring both categories of ware closer in their relationship to glass — that is the more glass a ware has in it — the easier it will be to flake off a chip because the harder the article is the more brittle it is.

## Stability of the Mending Material

When viewing the damage, you may have to consider a method of restoration as the most suitable for your article. However, unless indicated, Kay-O-lin may be used satisfactorily to repair most damages to pottery and stoneware in combination with such bonding material as Seal All, an Allen Products Corporation product. Seal-All is clear and in application does not yield to the porosity of pottery. Nor does Kay-O-lin. After bonding with Seal-All the cracks in the article may be sealed and concealed by using Kay-O-lin.

## Damage # 1

*Once cured, apply a coating of New Gloss Glaze.*

# DAMAGE # 1: SURFACE FLAKE DAMAGE; POTTERY AND STONEWARE

This is the same type of damage that occurs to china or glassware. Small pieces of an article are chipped off the top surface and lost. Usually the damage does not go through to the underside of the article. If the article is ironstone or pottery, use Seal All to bond the pieces. Use Kay-O-lin to seal the cracks.

1. Mix equal parts of Kay-O-lin putty-clay resin and hardener. Color to match existing. Use Grumbacher Oil paints. Make a firm putty mix.

2. Fill in the damage by pressing the putty mix down into the area that has flaked out and smooth with your finger until edges are even with existing.

3. Carefully smooth away excess, and clean surrounding surfaces with paper napkin dipped in acetone or lacquer thinner. Material will harden into stone in a matter of minutes. Therefore, it must be cleaned up while it is still soft as it is irremovable once it hardens. Do not get this material on your clothing.

4. Actual mending time, 5 minutes. However, it is well to let almost any type of mending set overnight for a lasting bond and cure.

5. Be sure you have cleaned all filminess and all excess from surrounding surfaces of the article before letting the putty mix set for cure. Once cured, apply a coating of New Glaze, which will help invisibilize the mend and blend with surrounding glazed surfaces.

    If surfaces are unglazed, do not apply glaze.

# DAMAGE # 2: SURFACE FLAKE OR EDGE CHIP; POTTERY

1. Prepare mix of Kay-O-lin putty-clay resin and hardener. Make a firm paste. Color to match pottery article.

2. Fill chip or flaked off edge chip.

3. Use art brush to press into all crevices.

4. Dampen fingers in water, and smooth away excess. Use paper napkin to clean surrounding surfaces. Leave no traces of clay on existing surfaces as it is irremovable when once hardened.

5. If damaged area is deep, apply two or three thin layers.

6. Balance article in sandbox. Allow drying time of 45 minutes.

7. Match and mix final shade of color with New Gloss Glaze.

8. If pottery article is unglazed, you will not need to use New Gloss Glaze.

Mending time: 5 minutes. Curing time 45 minutes. Recommended curing time: overnight.

# DAMAGE # 3: EDGE CHIP OR LIP CHIP WITH PIECE MISSING; POTTERY AND STONEWARE

This damage that occurs when one or two pieces in the shape of a "V" or wedge are broken out of the side or lip edge of an article of pottery or stoneware. The piece is missing. Backup support of masking tape is required, to keep the putty-clay in place.

1. Apply masking tape across the underside of the open "V" area. Reinforce until it is firm and you are sure it will not sag.

2. Follow steps 3 through 8 in preceding instruction for Damage # 2. After hardening:

9. Make sure all edges blend in with surrounding surfaces.

10. Sand gently until even with surrounding surfaces.

11. Reapply final coating of putty-clay and smooth out the edges until the matching repair is so well blended with existing that the repair is practically invisibilized. Let is stand and cure.

12. Apply final coating of New Gloss Glaze if required.

# DAMAGE # 4: BROKEN OUT PIECE; STONEWARE, OR HARD PASTE POTTERY

Chips and pieces broken off plates and similar articles of stoneware or hard paste pottery, also pieces broken off handles, spouts, the bottoms of cups,and other articles.

1. Study the section or piece which needs to be restored. The missing piece can be restored with Kay-O-lin. Or if you have the piece, it can be cemented into place using any of the above mentioned instant bonding materials. (These will not work on porous, soft-paste pottery.)

2. Mix just enough resin and hardener in equal parts to simulate the missing piece. Set aside.

3. Use masking tape to provide support across the open "V" or place where the piece is missing.

4. Fill in with putty-clay, colored to match surrounding.

5. When the putty-clay has set, discard the masking tape support.

6. Using a small square of sand paper, smooth edges until all edges are set in a smooth join.

7. Mix a fresh batch of putty, and surface coat over entire mend in order to unify all edges and invisibilize. Clay should be colored with Grumbacher Oil paints to match existing article.

8. Dampen your fingers with lacquer thinner and smooth away excess. (You will not be able to use water because you have used oil paints to color your putty-clay.)

9. Balance in sandbox and set aside to dry and harden. Mending time 10 minutes. Curing time, overnight.

10. When hard and set, complete your painting and coloring to match surrounding area, and use New Gloss Glaze for a final coating, if required.

# DAMAGE # 5: A BROKEN ARTICLE, SUCH AS A LAMP; HARD PASTE POTTERY

A lamp must be completely dismantled — everything removed from the pottery or stoneware body of the lamp —before repair is undertaken.

1. Inspect the surface damages to see if there are additional spider line cracks and chips. These damages must also be repaired in accordance with procedures set forth under respective headings in this chapter.

2. If a leaf or flower decoration has been broken off the side of the lamp, this can be re-applied by using one of the above listed instant bonding materials.

3. However, if the surface damage is small and part of the decoration, prepare equal parts of Kay-O-lin putty clay, and apply one layer at a time, permitting time for each layer to harden between applications. The clay must be mixed with Grumbacher Oil paint to match existing. Entire damage can be concealed and the cement evened off by dampening your fingers in acetone or lacquer thinner to wipe away excess. Final cleaning must be done with a paper napkin or piece of cheesecloth.

4. Bond broken pieces of the lamp with above listing instant bonding materials. Any of those mentioned will do.

5. Prepare mix of colored putty clay and apply to conceal all cracks and mended lines.

6. Permit this mix to begin to set up, then apply lacquer thinner with a piece of cheesecloth or dampened with acetone to wipe away excess, using a feathering out motion to even out and match material with surrounding areas.

7. Apply final coat of New Gloss Glaze.

8. Set in sandbox to harden and dry. Set time about 10 minutes. Curing time overnight.

# Damage # 5

# Damage # 6

### HOW TO RESTORE A STONEWARE STEIN WITH A LARGE CHIP MISSING OUT OF THE BASE.

*The missing chip presents a problem of whether to use a handgrinder to make a grid footing in which to anchor the mending material. To do so would involve technical problems. Let's do it the simple way. Working time is approximately 15 to 30 minutes. Curing time is overnight.*

# DAMAGE # 6: A BROKEN OR CHIPPED OUT BASE; POTTERY STEIN, MUG, OR VASE

You may have a large stoneware stein with a large chip missing out of the base. The missing chip presents a problem of whether to follow the professional method of using a hand grinder to make a grid footing in which to anchor the mending material. To do so would involve technical problems and considerable mending time. So let us try it the simple way, using Kay-O-lin putty-clay, colored to match the mug. Color your clay mix with Grumbacher Oil paints, blend by dampening your fingers in acetone or lacquer thinner. Working time to make this mend is approximately 15 to 20 minutes. Curing time, overnight, or 24 hours.

1. Mix equal parts of Kay-O-lin resin and hardener putty-clay.

2. When you have a firm paste, color with Grumbacher Oil paint, until you blended the clay mix to match the stein.

3. Apply material. Thumb-press; smooth out roughness. Dampen fingers dipped in acetone or lacquer thinner. If clay matches material without using oil paints, you may use water to smooth out roughness. (See page 114)

4. Use brush to blend material to surrounding areas. Resmooth with outward sweep of dampened fingertips (called feathering out) until all material is blended and mend is invisibilized.

5. Coat with New Gloss Glaze, using an art brush.

# Damage # 6

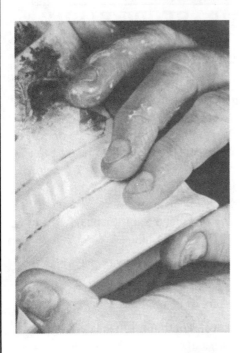

*Apply material. Thumb-press; smooth out roughness with fingers dipped in water. Use water very sparingly.*

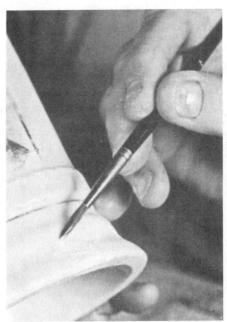

*Use brush to blend material to surrounding areas. Resmooth with outward sweep of dampened fingertips (feathering out).*

# DAMAGE # 7: A LID WITH A BROKEN FINIAL, POTTERY, STONEWARE, IRONSTONE

1. If the finial is missing, you may be able to mold a finial by hand.

2. Prepare Kay-O-lin resin and hardener putty clay in equal parts and mix into a firm ball, rolled in your hand. Add a proper base to fit the place where the finial is missing. Color with Grumbacher Oil paints.

3. If the hole goes clear through the lid, prepare lengths of masking tape and apply to the underside of the lid to cover the hole. Be sure clay matches.

4. Blend and firmly press clay mix into the hole and surrounding edges, until the base you are preparing will take a stem or upright piece of clay as a proper support for the clay ball, which is to serve as a finial. Allow set time of 45 minutes.

5. Prepare the stem support for the finial. Shape and blend into the base. Between each procedure with the clay, you must allow at least 45 minutes setting time, so that you can be assured of a firm structure. Permit stem to set.

6. Apply the ball of clay or finial. You may have given this top piece a bit of shaping such as shown in the illustration. After application, permit finial to set overnight.

7. Remove excess cement. If edges are showing, mix additional quantity of putty-clay, colored to match existing and blend in over all exposed edge. Apply evenly all around the mend, using your fingers dipped in acetone or lacquer thinner.

8. Remove excess. This is extremely important as Kay-O-lin will harden into a stone-like substance, and once married to the article, it is irremovable without damage to the appearance to the mend.

9. Apply New Gloss Glaze to finish coating the mend.

# DAMAGE # 8: A HOLE IN THE BASE OR SIDE OF A VASE; POTTERY OR STONEWARE

1. If the vase is large enough for your hand to be inserted inside, apply masking tape over the hole from the inside.

2. Prepare a mix of equal parts of resin and hardener Kay-O-lin, and color the clay mix with Grumbacher Oil paints to match existing article.

3. Be sure your masking tape is securely anchored on the inside. Anchor the tape well beyond the hole, so that it will fully cover the hole.

4. Anchor the tape to each side, well beyond the hole, beginning at the bottom and add additional lengths of the tape permitting one piece to overlay some of the one in place, until the hole is fully covered and the tape is well bonded and firmly in place.

5. Fill the hole with the putty-clay mix, and leave the article balanced in the sandbox to cure.

6. Allow 24 hours for curing. Actual mending time: 20 minutes.

7. If the mend is a particularly troublesome one, do not hesitate to use masking tape over the filled hole. The outside tape, thus applied, will support and hold the material in place while it is hardening.

8. When dry and hard, remove tapes, and smooth surfaces with a bit of fine sandpaper.

9. Apply one or two coats of the clay mix, thinned to a slurry.

10. If the pottery stoneware is colored, add color as required to the mix to match existing.

11. Coat surrounding surfaces of mended article by perfectly matching clay mix to existing. Feather out material by spreading or thinning. Keep fingers dampened in acetone or lacquer thinner while stroking and blending.

12. Apply finishing coat of New Gloss Glaze.

# DAMAGE # 9: A BROKEN SPOUT ON A POT OR PITCHER; POTTERY, STONEWARE

1. First, clean the pot thoroughly.

2. Dry, and inspect damage for cracks extending from broken lip of spout down into pieces to be repaired.

3. Plan assembly of all broken pieces.

4. Prepare Kay-O-lin mix of equal parts of the resin and hardener, and color the mix to match article to be mended. Use Grumbacher Oil paint and blend color into the mix until you have a perfect match.

5. Prepare strips of masking tape in lengths needed to secure any pieces to be cemented together.

6. Apply any instant bonding material such as Krazy Glue to join the broken pieces. Mending time 15 minutes.

7. Take a razor blade and scrape off any excess. Moisten in acetone or lacquer thinner to make the work easier and quicker.

8. Attach broken off spout to coffee pot. Use an instant bonding material such as Krazy Glue, and permit the mend to "set" for a few minutes.

9. Remove any excess glue that has hardened around the mend by using a razor blade dipped in acetone or lacquer thinner.

10. You are now ready to use putty mix to model and reshape the damaged lip. Prepare a base or supporting mold with strips of masking tape, applied to the underside of the place to be mended. Form a lip or pouring spout with the putty mix, and model this carefully. Give it a slight trough in the middle to provide good pouring.

11. Smooth and shape the putty mix until you have unified the clay with all edges.

12. Let set for 24 hours. Remove tapes.

13. Remove excess with a razor blade or sand with sandpaper until smooth and well blended with existing. Glaze with New Gloss Glaze. Set aside to dry.

# DAMAGE # 10: A BROKEN HANDLE; POTTERY STONEWARE, IRONSTONE

Soft paste pottery, the kind made of soft paste or material such as firebrick is very porous and presents grave difficulty when it comes to bonding as materials such as Krazy Glue, Super Glue, Perma-bond, and others are simply absorbed into the edges of the article and will not bond. However, after two or three applications of the material, apply again to all broken edges. Work with your largest pieces first, then tape each piece together, working from the largest to the smallest. Allow drying time of 30 minutes or so. Chances are you can now safely remove the tape and the pieces will adhere to one another. No guarantee. But you may have luck. If not, you still have to use a bonding material such as Stix All and follow the masking tape procedure taping the largest pieces together and working down to the smallest as you go. You will have to allow the assembled pieces to set overnight for the bonding to cure.

1. Balance your article on its side in the sand box.

2. Apply bonding material to top and bottom edges of the broken handle and to the nubs on the broken article.

3. Press firmly into place, keeping handle upright. Hold until bond has taken hold. Permit drying time of a few seconds.

4. Remove excess glue. Use razor blade dipped in acetone or lacquer thinner.

5. Prepare Kay-O-lin mix in equal parts of resin and hardener, and color with Grumbacher Oil paints to match broken article.

6. Apply putty-clay mix around top and bottom mend spots where handle is joined to broken article.

7. Use an art brush to blend in over mended edges. Dip and moisten brush in acetone or lacquer thinner all the time blending, thinning, spreading out the clay mix to conceal the mend and invisibilize the work.

8. Apply coating of New Gloss Glaze. Blend with existing surrounding surfaces.

# DAMAGE # 11: HAIRLINE CRACKS; POTTERY, STONEWARE, IRONWARE

## Statement of the Problem

Getting ready to boil your cracked article: First examine the edges. Are the edges of the crack tight together or can you insert a razor blade between them? Is the crack dirty, and discolored, or are the edges aged and crumbly? Whether the edges are tight together or loose, boil out any possible discoloration and dirt, using a safe bleaching agent, such as Clorox. Tri-sodium phosphate works very well. Use an enamel pan or bucket big enough and deep enough to enable you to submerge the article. The cracked part must be completely covered. After the crack is truly clean and seems to have disappeared, air dry it and treat the crack(s) as follows:

1. Determine whether the crack is tight or loose; that is decide whether edges can be spread apart or are immovable.

2. After boiling and bleaching procedures outlined above, permit article to dry thoroughly. Overnight if possible.

3. Reinspect. Continue boiling process if discoloration has not disappeared. Do not dilute the bleach.

4. When article is ready, prepare clay mix of equal parts of resin and hardener. Insert a knife blade or razor's edge into open end of crack to open it wider. Wiggle the blade in. But do not press or force. Apply the clay mix to fill the crack, and smooth evenly in a blend with existing.

5. Moisten your fingers in acetone or lacquer thinner as you work, to press in the cement.

6. Feather-out the edges until all surplus is removed and the filling is even with adjoining surfaces.

7. Set aside to dry.

8. Apply coating of New Gloss Glaze.

# CHAPTER TEN:
# INSTANT MENDING OF
# JEWELRY: STEP-BY-STEP

# NOTES ABOUT JEWELRY

Jewelry has many aspects such as value as well as fashion. Style also is an aspect of jewelry because style often helps to show what we are like and what we admire. The most charming pieces of jewelry are sometimes carved stone animal and bird weights and pendants. Present ideas of fashion in jewelry include beads of lapis lazuli, carnelian, agate, pearls, and semi-precious stones, even glass.

The only kind of jewelry we can mend with instant mending material will be stones and enamels applied to metal forms, such as those shown in the illustration. Instant mending materials will not mend broken metal. Broken metal chains, wings, feet, claws, heads, and the like will require the expertise of a jeweler. But it is possible with instant mending materials to simulate enameling and to replace broken cameos, and stone or enameled pieces. These pieces can be successfully reglued to metal backing if they have come loose.

# DAMAGE # 1: WING BROKEN OFF METAL BODY OF A SCARAB (EGYPTIAN BEETLE)

1. Examine damage and assess gluing surface.

2. Clean and dry surfaces. Remove any soap, oil, dirt, grease, or old glue.

3. Apply a thin coat of Seal All or Adhesive (a silicone rubber cement) to the surface of the broken article. A very thin layer covering one surface only, is sufficient. If you are using Adhesive, the vinegar-like odor, present during application, disappears as the material cures.

4. Fit pieces firmly together and squeeze out any excess materials, to allow reassembly of all pieces. Be careful not to squeeze out all of the Adhesive.

5. Support the two broken pieces to stay together by using a wooden clothespin. Clamp them together.

6. Permit "set" to cure. Takes about 5 minutes.

7. Remove any excess material. Use razor blade dipped in acetone.

8. Re-enamel with New Gloss Glaze.

# DAMAGE # 2: LAVA JEWELRY

1. Lava jewelry pieces can be restored by use of Kay-O-lin putty-clay, colored with Grumbacher Oil paints to match the broken article.

2. Because of the porousity of lava, use ADHESIVE to cement your broken pieces together. If they are chipped or a piece is missing, rebuild same by using Kay-O-lin colored clay, to match existing.

3. If the work is intricate, make sure all pieces are re-assembled and firmly attached to the metal ring, brooch, locket, pin, or backing from which they broke loose. For intricate work, use very small quantities of the clay and rebuild the chipped out area, or missing piece with a toothpick. You can do it, with this material and patience.

4. Normally, adhesive takes about 5 minutes to "set" and 24 hours to cure into a firm bond. When you are working with jewelry, take your time, step-by-step for lasting satisfactory results.

5. The bonding of broken pieces always comes first. The rebuilding of stone or lava pieces of jewelry follows after the bonding.

6. For 3 dimensional effects, use Kay-O-lin clay colored with Grumbacher Oil paints to match existing.

7. Final enameled effect may be achieved by use of New Gloss Glaze. Apply sparingly with art brush.

8. Set aside to dry, and allow at least 24 hours for cure.

# DAMAGE # 3: ENAMELING, CLOISONNE EFFECT; CHIPPED OUT PIECES

1. Prepare 50/50 mix of E-Pox-E glue.

2. Color with Grumbacher Oil paint to match enamel area to be mended.

3. Thin material with lacquer thinner or acetone as required, to prevent too rapid a "set" of mending material.

4. Apply material a spare drop at a time, with an art brush. Moisten your art brush in acetone or lacquer thinner before beginning application, so that the brush will work easily with the material as you apply it.

5. Be very careful not to use excess of material. Excess can and must be removed immediately with your art brush, as it will "set" almost immediately.

6. If you would feel more comfortable working with a slower curing material, look for an epoxy resin and hardener, two part system that takes longer. You will undoubtedly find such a material at your local hardware store, on a hang-up card in the section where they have instant mending materials. The card will state the length of curing time the material takes.

7. However, an epoxy resin and hardener system that has a delayed "setting" time may be runny and much more difficult to work with than the faster curing material.

8. Whichever you use, the enameling effect can be achieved. Allow adequate curing time.

9. Apply final coating of New Gloss Glaze.

10. Permit curing time of 24 hours.

# DAMAGE # 4: RE-ENAMELING BROKEN OUT PIECES OF ENAMEL

1. Epoxy White Resin Paste has not been mentioned before for instant mending, as it is a paste that must be used with a slow curing two part epoxy resin and hardener system that is perfectly clear.

2. Many different kinds of mending can be done with this "three" part system as the white paste can be colored to match whatever is to be mended and once added to the resin and hardener, will give off a jeweled, enameled effect.

3. Epoxy White Resin Paste may be obtained from the author, and is particularly useful in re-enameling Cloisonne objects of art as well as jewelry.

4. Any of the wings of insects shown as well as the flower petals of such jewelry used in the illustration can be restored to a beautiful re-enameled condition by using the suggested three-part system.

5. In every case, it is essential first to clean, and carefully remove every scrap and shred of broken enamel still clinging to the metal backing.

6. If the wing or flower petal is multicolored or multi-faceted, you will have to enamel one section or area at a time. Permit curing time between each mending operation.

7. Prepare a mix of equal parts of the epoxy resin and hardener. Stir thoroughly with a wooden probe stick, wooden match stick, or tongue depressor. Add small quantities of the Epoxy White resin paste until you have the right consistency of a drop of enamel.

8. If the enameling job requires colored enamel, mix the Epoxy White resin paste with Grumbacher Color to match the area to be mended prior to adding it to the resin and hardener.

9. Apply the simulated epoxy enamel drop by drop with an art brush until the mending area is all filled in. Permit curing time of 24 hours.

# APPENDICES

# APPRAISAL RESOURCES AND PRICE GUIDE BOOKS FOR YOUR GLASS, CHINA, & COLLECTIBLES

Andacht, Sandra. *Treasury of Satsuma,* Wallace-Homestead, Dubuque, IA.

Archer, Mary and Douglas. *Collectible Glass Candlesticks,* Collector's Books, Paducah, KY, 1984.

Battie, Michael and Turner. *Price Guide to 19th & 20th Century Porcelain,* Apollo Books, Poughkeepsie, NY, 1984.

Bishop & Ketchum. *The Knopf Collector's Price Guide to Antique Glass and China,* Alfred Knopf, New York, NY, 1984.

Bishop & Ketchum. *The Knopf Collector's Guide to Glass Tableware, Bowls and Vases,* Alfred Knopf, New York, NY, 1983.

Edwards, Bill. *Price Guide to Carnival Glass,* Collector's Books, Paducah, KY, 1983.

Evers, Jo Ann. *Cut Glass Value Guide,* Collector's Books, Paducah, KY, 1984.

Metz, Alice. *Price Guide to Early American Pattern Glass,* Spencer, Walker, Columbus, OH.

Huxford's 2nd Edition, *Roseville Pottery, with Value Guide,* Collector's Books, Paducah, KY.

King, Constance. *Price Guide to Dolls,* Apollo Books, Poughkeepsie, NY, 1983.

Koch, Robt. *Louis C. Tiffany Glass, Bronzes and Lamps,* Crown Publishers, NY.

Lyle's Series on Collectibles with Current Values, Apollo Books, Poughkeepsie, NY.

Mackay, David. *Price Guide to More Collectibles,* Apollo Books, Poughkeepsie, NY.

Miller's *Price Guide to Glass and China,* Professional Handbook, Apollo Books, Poughkeepsie, NY, 1982.

Mount, Sally. *Price Guide to English Pottery,* Apollo Books, Poughkeepsie, NY.

Pearson, J. Michael. *Encyclopedia of American Cut and Engraved Glass,* Miami Beach, Florida (Published by Pearson), 1984. Volumes I, II, and III.

Peterson, Harold. *How Do You Know It's Old?* Charles Schribner, New York, NY, 1980.

Revi, A. C. *19th Century Glass,* Thos. Nelson, New York.

Taylor & Hart. *China Painting Step by Step,* Van Nostrand, New York.

Van Patten, Joan. *Price Guide to Collectible Nippon China,* Collector's Books, Paducah, KY.

Gavston, Mary Frank. *Flow Blue China,* Collector's Books, Paducah, KY.

Young, Harriet. *Grandmother's Haviland, with Price Guide,* Wallace-Homestead, Dubuque, IA.

# MAJOR MANUFACTURERS OF PORCELAIN, CHINA, AND POTTERY

## ORIENTAL PORCELAIN

*China-Trade Porcelain*
(Chinaware made and decorated in China according to Western design and decoration, chiefly in 18th century)

*Oriental Export Porcelain*
(Includes all chinaware made in the Orient for export, chiefly to Europe, in 18th century)

*Oriental Lowestoft*
(A misnomer sometimes used to describe Oriental Export chinaware. Has no connection with English Lowestoft)

*Imari*
(Japanese porcelain, made from 17th century. Inferior in quality to China-Trade porcelain, but more elaborately decorated, sometimes using gold decoration)

*Kakiemon*
(Japanese porcelain, made from 17th century, exported through port of Arita)

*Nankin (Nankeen)*
*Canton*
*Rose Medallion*
(Types of Oriental Export Porcelain, made chiefly in early 19th century)

*Dynastic Chinaware*
(Porcelain made in China from 8th and 9th centuries according to Chinese design and for Chinese use only. Dynastic decorations)

## EUROPEAN CHINAWARE

*Meissen*
(Made at royal factory in Meissen from 1710 into early 19th century)

| | |
|---|---|
| *Böttger* | 1710–1719 |
| *Höroldt-Kändler* | 1720–1745 |
| *Rococo* | 1745–1774 |
| *Marcolini* | 1774 1814 |

*Dresden*
(Term in use today to describe porcelain made in other factories in Dresden)

Other German factories making hard paste chinaware in 18th century. Known today by name of city where manufactured:

| | Founded c. |
|---|---|
| *Höchst* | 1746 |
| *Nymphenburg* | 1747 |
| *Berlin (Wegeley)* | 1751 |
| *Fürstenberg* | 1753 |
| *Frankenthal* | 1755 |
| *Ludwigsburg* | 1756 |

Austria
| | |
|---|---|
| *Vienna* | 1718 |

France
| Soft Paste | |
|---|---|
| *Rouen* | 1763 |
| *St.-Cloud* | 1702–1765 |
| *Mennecy-Villeroy* | 1748 |
| *Vincennes* | 1745 |
| *Sevres* | 1745–1769 |

| Soft Paste and Hard Paste | |
|---|---|
| *Sevres* | 1769 to 1800 |

| Hard Paste | |
|---|---|
| *Sevres* | after 1800 |

## EUROPEAN CHINAWARE (cont.)

Denmark
 *Royal Copenhagen* from 1773

Italy
   Hard Paste
 *Venice*  from about 1720

   Soft Paste
 *Capo-di-Monte* as early as 1743

Spain
   Soft Paste
 *Buen Retiro*  from 1757

*English Chinaware*
   Soft Paste
Made in these factories up to the introduction of hard paste about 1770.
*Chelsea*
*Derby*
*Bow*
*Bristol*
*Worcester*
*Spode*
*Minton*
*Lowestoft*
*Caughley*
*Coalport*

   Hard Paste
*"Cookworthy's Plymouth,"* first hard paste china made in England about 1770. Thereafter, most of the factories made some hard paste chinaware.

*Bone China:* This type of chinaware was developed between 1790–1810. Thereafter, most English factories began using this type, and it is the principal type of English china made today. Familiar names: *Spode, Worcester Royal Porcelain, Royal Crown Derby.*

## AMERICAN CHINAWARE

*Pickard Inc.*
 (Level with Lenox)
*Buffalo China Co.*
 (vitreous)
*American Haviland & Company*
*Iroquois China — Syracuse China Co.*
*Hyalyn Porcelain Ware*
*Crooksville China Co.*
*Hall China Co.*
*Laughlin-Homer Co.*
*Salem China Co.*
*French Saxon Co.*
*Royal China Co.*
*Chenango Ceramics*
*Cordey*
*Atlas Crystal and Commemorative Porcelain Co.*
*Sun Prairie Porcelains*
*Lenox*

## ENGLISH POTTERY

Hard paste

*Burslem*
 (Ironstone)
*Caughley Fenton*
 (Mason)
*Whieldon*
*Fulham*
*Lambeth*
*Doulton*
*Herculaneum*
*Cauldon*
*Imperial Stone*
*Staffordshire*
*Minton*
*Spode*
*Swansea*
*Rockingham*
*Wedgwood*
*Etruria*
*Worcester*

| EUROPEAN POTTERY | AMERICAN POTTERY |
|---|---|
| **Hard and/or Soft Paste** | **Hard and/or Soft Paste** |

| | |
|---|---|
| Belgium | East Liverpool |
| *Liege* | *Ironstone* |
| *Copenhagen* | Greenpoint |
| *Naestved Danish* | *Faience* |
| *China Works* | Birmington, VT |
| France | *Fenton* |
| *Aprey* | Glasgow, NJ |
| *Apt* | *Potterwares* |
| *Blois* | Globe |
| *Lille* | *Earthenwares* |
| *Sarreguemines* | *Ironstones* |
| *Sceaux* | Grueby |
| *Sèvres Biscuit* | *Faience* |
| Germany | Knowles, Taylor |
| *Bernburg* | *Stoneware* |
| *Damm* | *Ironstone* |
| *Diemstein* | *Semi Porcelain* |
| *Mettlach* | John Maddock |
| *Minden* | *Ironstone* |
| Poland | Akron |
| *Stawsk* | *Ironstone* |
| Spain | Jersey City |
| *Faience* | *American* |
| *Majolica* | *Pottery* |
| Holland | *Ironstone* |
| *Delft* | Trenton, NJ |
| Italy | *Anchor* |
| *Semi Porcelain* | *Earthenware* |
| *Faenza* | Buffalo Pottery |
| *Majolica* | *Ironstone* |
| *Forli* | Chesapeake |
| *Capo di Monte* | *(Severn)* |
| *Genoa* | *Earthenwares* |
| Norway | Phoenixville |
| *Luxembourg* | *Slipwares* |
| Sweden | *Earthenwares* |
| *Fayence* | Crescent |
| Russia | *Ironstone* |
| *St. Petersburg* | *Semi-Porcelain* |
| *Moscow* | Crown Pottery |
| *Kiev* | *Semi Vitreous* |
| | *Faience* |

| AMERICAN POTTERY (cont.)<br>Hard and/or Soft Paste | ORIENTAL POTTERY<br>Hard and/or Soft Paste |
|---|---|
| Matt Morgan<br>*Art Pottery* | Japan<br>*Dai Nippon*<br>*Kutani* |
| New England Pottery<br>*Art Pottery*<br>*Stoneware* | *Ya Yoi*<br>*Hawiwa* |
| Ott & Brewer<br>*"Belleek"* | |
| Onondaga Pottery<br>*Syracuse*<br>*Ironstone* | |
| Rookwood<br>*Ironstone*<br>*Faience*<br>*Earthenwares*<br>*Art Wares* | |
| Sebring<br>*Stoneware* | |
| Trenton<br>*Tiles* | |
| Weller<br>*Earthenwares* | |
| Wheeling<br>*Earthenwares* | |

# DIRECTORY OF MARKS FOUND ON POTTERY & PORCELAIN

## MARKS ON POTTERY OF ITALY

# MARKS ON WARES OF ITALY, PERSIA, RHODES, ETC.

## MARKS ON POTTERY OF FRANCE

CH

J. Boulard a Nevers
1822

ILF
1636

M.C.A 1756.J.A

P.F.

HB     H.B     P.C     E.Borne     de conrad
1689   1689                1689      A neuers

.F.R.1734   N   R.+ Limoges ◆
                Le 18ᵐᵉ may
                J74J

de Conrade
a nuers

avisseau
a tour
1855

A:C
A

AN

A
P.

A
E

CD
CABRI   ℛ   CB   C.S.   ꝺ   F   F.C- 1661
1762

GDG   ⨸FG ⨸SG   FE.   ſſ.   GAA   Hi
1780
½   "Fait par GDE, A⁻ 1761."   HE   H G i

N.Jamac   H   G/H   ·II·   J   JB
1696

🌸   Lejeune·   A.R.   F   R
·Leger·   ·1730·

M   NICOLas H.V   OIP, OP
1738

OS   I·R·Paivadeavt   PB   P   P₄
1643

P   GP   P   PO   P·R·

PV   R   R   R.B F   RL
3l2

R·M· F   s· G· h·   NE   T.C.L
1793 un 41

·VM   W²   W   W H   ·P·

## MARKS ON POTTERY OF BELGIUM AND HOLLAND

6※　　※ℜ　　※ G　　$\overline{\dfrac{CCC}{C.B}}$　　·IM·　　ℱP

ℬ　　B.L　　　　　CA　　　　i

F 1677　　E 1.6.8.0　　R G　　MD Sloot 1720　　Jr G

127 D·G　　GH VP 160　　　　SE 50　　VE 24

VP　　5⌐2f⌐　　　　　AK

IE　　°W　　$\dfrac{PVM}{48}$　　WK　　$\dfrac{MP}{9}$　　DRN 2

Hauw　　I D M　　　　CPC　　PSA　　AK

$\dfrac{AK}{\dfrac{145}{146}}{268}$　　HK　　ES　　xfurtuyn　　WVDB

IB　　D°　　*130　　AK　　AK　　I D A　　❀ DVD

Roos　　D　　$\dfrac{L.S}{7}$　　♦♦♦　　WD　　$\dfrac{ITD}{12}$

DEX     Z :DEX.     I Π D     Hooren     M

$$\frac{18}{2}$$

VC     E. B. S     CVS     GVS     RS

Γ     bq     JB     HVMD

$$5$$

THART     thart     R     $\frac{B}{2}$     Duijn

youjn     vduijn     De Blompot     PD

D. S. K     el kan     LPK     (Pt     W. V. B.

## UNKNOWN MARKS ON POTTERY OF HOLLAND

# MARKS ON POTTERY OF GERMANY, SWEDEN, DENMARK, SPAIN AND PORTUGAL

B/Z    Z    A:B 1638    Matthias Rosa im. Anspach    B.K.    BK/C

BP    BP B.P BP    ‡    ℛ    A/F    H

göggingen HS    S.    G    JZ    ✹    ⚓

G:Koxdenbusch.    GK:    A    NB./K::    NB/F    NB::/4.

Stebner 1775 d.13 8bris    S    E/v8    F. 20/T · E 68.P.F. Hm    E+ D. 11/4 10

H A    B/S    DP/83X    F.B.C.F. 1779    GHEDT W:1:M J1730    H/S

A/P/MR    :HS:    HK N    HN XX    HN XX    ·J

R/N    OF    F. Rahl:. AS:1796:.    PH    N Pössinger Anno 1725

K/M/67    R·M/E    S.    K B B    VH/3

W    Y    WR    ♡    ⚜    xsa

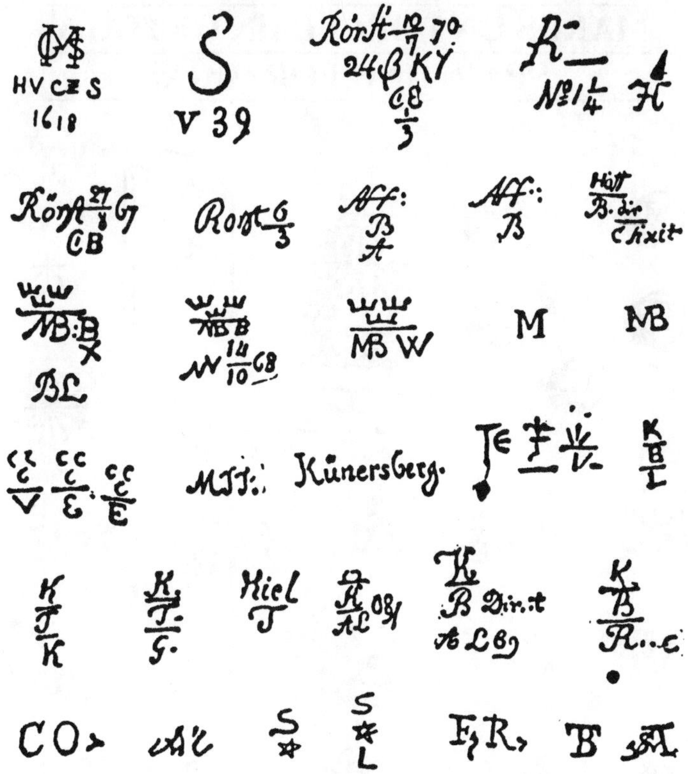

# MARKS ON PORCELAIN OF ITALY, SPAIN AND PORTUGAL

## MARKS ON PORCELAIN OF SEVRES

# MARKS USED BY PAINTERS, DECORATORS AND GILDERS AT SEVRES

## FIRST PERIOD. 1753–1799

*Aloncle*—birds, animals, emblems, etc.

*Antcaume*—landscape, animals.

*Armand*—birds, flowers, etc.

*Asselin*—portraits, miniatures, etc.

*Aubert* (senior)—flowers.

*Bailly* (son)—flowers.

*Bardet*—flowers.

*Barre*—detached bouquets.

*Barrat*—garlands, bouquets.

*Baudoin*—ornaments, friezes, etc.

*Becquet*—flowers, etc.

*Bertrand*—detached bouquets.

*Bienfait*—gilding.

*Binet*—detached bouquets.

*Binet, Madame* (née *Sophie Chanou*)—flowers.

*Boucher*—flowers, garlands, etc.

*Bouchet*—landscape, figures, ornaments.

*Bouillat*—flowers, landscapes.

*Boulanger*—detached bouquets.

*Boulanger* (son)—pastoral subjects, children.

*Bulidon*—detached bouquets.

*Bunel, Madame* (née *Manon Buteux*)—flowers.

*Couturier*—gilding.

*Dieu*—Chinese, Chinese flowers, gilding, etc.

*Dodin*—figure, various subjects, portraits.

*Drand*—Chinese, gilding.

*Dubois*—flowers, garlands, etc.

*Dusolle*—detached bouquets, etc.

*Dutanda*—detached bouquets, garlands.

*Evans*—birds, butterflies, landscapes.

*Falot*—arabesques, birds, butterflies.

*Fontaine*—emblems, miniatures, etc.

*Bunel, Madame*—another form.

*Buteux* (senior)—flowers, emblems, etc.

*Buteux* (elder son)—detached bouquets, etc.

*Buteux* (younger son)—pastoral subjects, children.

*Capel*—friezes.

*Cardin*—detached bouquets.

*Carrier*—flowers.

*Castel*—landscapes, hunts, birds.

*Caton*—pastoral subjects, children, birds.

*Catrice*—flowers, detached bouquets.

*Chabry*—miniatures, pastoral subjects.

*Chanou, Madame* (née *Julie Durosey*)—flowers.

*Chapuis* (elder)—flowers, birds, etc.

*Chapuis* (younger)—detached bouquets.

*Chauvaux* (father)—gilding.

*Chauvaux* (son)—detached bouquets, gilding.

*Chevalier*—flowers, bouquets, etc.

*Cheusy, De*—flowers, arabesques.

*Chulot*—emblems, flowers, arabesques.

*Commelin*—detached bouquets, garlands.

*Cornaille*—flowers, detached bouquets.

*Henrion*—garlands, detached bouquets.

*Héricourt*—detached bouquets, garlands.

*Hilken*—figures, pastoral subjects, etc.

*Houry*—flowers, etc.

*Huny*—detached bouquets, flowers.

*Joyau*—detached bouquets, etc.

*Jubin*—gilding.

*La Roche*—flowers, garlands, emblems.

*La Roche*—another form.

*Le Bel* (elder)—figures and flowers.

♡ *Fontelliau*—gilding, etc.

Y *Fouré*—flowers, bouquets, etc.

※ *Fritsch*—figures, children.

*Fumez*—detached bouquets.

ƒ.x *Fumez*—another form.

*Gauthier*—landscape and animals.

G *Genest*—figure and genre.

✝ *Genin*—flowers, garlands, friezes, etc.

ℒd. *Gerard*—pastoral subjects, miniatures.

Y.t *Gerard, Madame (née Vautrin)*—flowers.

*Girard*—arabesques, Chinese, etc.

*Gomery*—flowers and birds.

ℊɣ *Gremont*—garlands, bouquets.

Ӿ *Grison*—gilding.

m *Michel*—detached bouquets.

M *Moiron*—detached bouquets; also another form used by Michel.

5. *Mongenot*—flowers, detached bouquets.

M *Morin*—marine, military subjects.

ʌ *Mutel*—landscape.

n q *Niquet*—detached bouquets, etc.

⟲ *Noel*—flowers, ornaments.

ᏚᎠ *Nouailhier, Madame (née Sophie Durosy)*—flowers.

Jp *Parpette*—flowers, detached bouquets.

L.S. *Parpette, Dlle. Louison*—flowers.

👁 *Pajou*—figure.

P.T. *Petit*—flowers.

ƒ *Pfeiffer*—detached bouquets.

ƒp.o *Pierre (elder)*—flowers, bouquets.

p.7 *Pierre (younger)*—bouquets, garlands.

P.H. *Philippine (elder)*—pastoral subjects, children, etc.

ℬ.t. *Pithou (elder)*—portraits, historical subjects.

ℬ.j. *Pithou (younger)*—figures, flowers, ornaments.

Ꝋ *Pouillot*—detached bouquets.

HP. *Prevost*—gilding.

❊... *Raux*—detached bouquets.

ℒℬ.. *Le Bel (younger)*—garlands, bouquets, etc.

✷ *Léandre*—pastoral subjects, miniatures.

ℒℒ *Lecot*—Chinese, etc.

LL *Lecot*—another form.

⌄ *Ledoux*—landscape and birds.

ℒℊ *Le Guay*—gilding.

LG *Le Guay*—another form.

Ꝙ *Leguay*—miniatures, children, Chinese.

ℒ or L *Levé (father)*—flowers, birds, arabesques.

f *Levé, Felix*—flowers, Chinese.

ℛ.ℬ *Maqueret, Madame (née Bouillat)*—flowers.

M *Massy*—groups of flowers, garlands.

ℐ *Merault (elder)*—friezes.

ℐ9 *Merault (younger)*—garlands, bouquets.

X *Micaud*—flowers, bouquets, medallions.

⚹ *Rochet*—figure, miniatures, etc.

⟋ *Rosset*—landscapes, etc.

ℛℒ. *Roussel*—detached bouquets.

S.h. *Schradre*—birds, landscape, etc.

❧ *Sinsson*—flowers, groups, garlands, etc.

∵ *Sioux (elder)*—detached bouquets, garlands.

◇ *Sioux (younger)*—flowers, garlands.

◇ *Tabary*—birds, etc.

✳ *Taillandier*—detached bouquets, garlands.

••• *Tandart*—groups of flowers, garlands.

⬭ *Tardi*—detached bouquets, etc.

•••• *Theodore*—gilding.

Ɉ *Thevenet (father)*—flowers, medallions, groups, etc.

Jt. *Thevenet (son)*—ornaments, friezes, etc.

V *Vaudé*—gilding, flowers.

W *Vavasseur*—arabesques.

⊔⊔ *Vieillard*—emblems, ornaments, etc.

2.000 *Vincent*—gilding.

✿ *Xrowet*—arabesques, flowers, etc.

↑ *Yvernel*—landscape, birds.

## SECOND PERIOD. 1800-1874

J.A — André, Jules—landscape.

R — Apoil—figures, subjects, etc.

E.R. — Apoil, Madame—figure.

B — Barré—flowers.

B. — Barriat—figure.

B.n — Beranger—figure.

B — Blanchard—decorator.

AB — Blanchard, Alex.—ornament worker.

B.t — Boitel—gilding.

B — Bonnuit—decorator.

B — Boullemier, Antoine—gilding.

J.B — Boullèmier (elder)—gilding.

Bf — Boullemier (son)—gilding.

Bx. — Buteux—flowers.

E — Cabau—flowers.

CP — Capronnier—gilding.

JC — Célos—ornament worker (pâtes sur pâtes).

LC — Charpentier—decorator.

J.C. — Charrin, Dlle. Fanny—subjects, figures, portraits.

C.C. — Constant—gilding.

C.t. — Constantin—figure.

D — Dammouse—figure, ornament (pâtes sur pâtes).

D — David—decorator.

D.F. — Delafosse—figure.

D.F. — Davignon—landscape.

D. — Desperais—ornaments.

DC — Derichsweiller—decorator.

CD — Develly—landscape and genre.

Dh — Deutsch—ornaments.

D.I. — Didier—ornaments, etc.

D: — Didier—another form.

A. — Martinet—flowers.

E.deM — Maussion, Mdlle. de—figure

M — Merigot—ornaments, etc.

MAR — Meyer, Alfred—figure, etc.

MC — Micaud—gilding.

M — Milet, Optat—decorator on faience and pastes.

A — Archelais—ornament worker (pâtes sur pâtes).

P.A — Avisse—ornament worker.

B — Barbin—ornaments.

D.t — Drouet—flowers.

AD — Ducluzeau, Madame—figure, subjects, portraits, etc.

Dy — Durosey—gilding.

HF — Farraguet, Madame—figure, subjects, etc.

F — Ficquenet—flowers and ornaments (pâtes sur pâtes).

F — Fontaine—flowers.

UN — Fragonard—figure, genre, etc.

Gu — Ganeau (son)—gilding.

J.G — Gély—ornament worker (pâtes sur pâtes).

J.J. — Georget—figure, portraits, etc.

G.ob.R — Gobert—figure on enamel and on pastes.

D.G. — Godin—gilding.

F.G. — Goupil—figure.

G — Guillemain—decorator.

H — Hallion, Eugène—landscape.

H — Hallion, François—decorator in gilding.

h.D. — Huard—ornaments, divers styles.

.Ch. — Humbert—figure.

E — Julienne—ornaments, style Renaissance, etc.

A — Lambert—flowers.

LGu — Langlacé—landscape.

I — Latache—gilding.

L.B. — Le Bel—landscape.

L — Legay—ornament worker (pâtes sur pâtes).

l.G. — Le Gay—figures, various subjects, portraits.

IG — Legrand—gilding.

EL — Leroy, Eugène—gilding.

R — Richard, François—decorator..

J.h.R — Richard, Joseph—decorator.

# — Richard, Paul—decorative gilding.

R. — Riocreux, Isidore—landscape.

Rx — Riocreux, Désiré-Denis—flowers.

| | |
|---|---|
| *MR* | *Moreau*—gilding. |
| AM | *Moriot*—figure, etc. |
| *PP* | *Parpette, Dlle.*—flowers. |
| *L.L.* | *Philippine*—flowers and ornaments. |
| P | *Pline*—decorative gilding. |
| *PR* | *Poupart*—landscape. |
| *R* | *Regnier, Ferd.*—figure, various subjects. |
| *JR* | *Regnier, Hyacinthe*—figure. |
| *JR* | *Rejoux*—decorator. |
| *E 1900* | *Renard, Émile*—decorator. |
| *EMR* | *Richard, Émile*—flowers. |
| *ER* | *Richard, Eugène*—flowers. |

| | |
|---|---|
| *PR* | *Robert, Pierre*—landscape. |
| *GR* | *Robert Madame*—flowers and landscape. |
| *R* | *Robert, Jean-François*—landscape. |
| *PMR* | *Roussel*—figure, etc. |
| *PS* | *Schilt, Louis-Pierre*—flowers. |
| *S.S.p* | *Sinsson* (father)—flowers. |
| *M* | *Solon*—figures and ornaments (pâtes sur pâtes). |
| *S.W.* | *Sweback*—landscape and genre. |
| *J.T.* | *Trager*—flowers, birds. |
| *T.* | *Troyon*—ornaments. |
| W | *Walter*—flowers. |

# UNDETERMINED SIGNATURES, ETC.

*W Yg CR* } Three marks on plate dated 1821, view of Moka, signed L. M., richly gilded. The first mark also on several plates dated 1812, lapis-lazuli borders, heavy gilding, antique cameo paintings.

*M* On richly decorated and gilded plates, 1821.

*Phim* On plate, time of Louis XVIII., richly gilded; monochrome portrait of Racine: (probable mark of Philippine.)

*Dm Rog* On plate not dated, rich gilding, monochrome portrait of Bourdaloue.

*BT* On fine plates and vases, 1812.

*Due Tre* On plate *temp* Louis XVIII., rich gilding, monochrome portrait of Bourdon (? Dlle. de Treverret).

*R* Twice this size on plate, 1822, view of Sèvres factory; possibly a *visa* of Riocreux.

*Lp* In black on foot of ice vase, with river deities in superb gilding, dated 1831.

# ARTISTS' SIGNATURES FOUND
# AT FULL LENGTH

*Baldisseroni*—figure.

*Brunel*—figure.

*Bulot*—flowers.

*Cool, Madame de*—figure.

*Courcy, De*—figure.

*Froment*—figure.

*Gallois, Madame (née Durand)*—figure.

*Garneray*—landscape.

*De Gault*—figure.

*Geddé*—decorator, enamels and relief.

*Hamon*—figure.

*Jaccober*—flowers and fruits.

*Jacquotot, Madame Victoire*—figure, subjects, portraits.

*Jadelot, Madame*—figure.

*Lamarre*—landscape.

*Langlois, Polycles*—landscape.

*Laurent, Madame Pauline*—figure, subjects, etc.

*Lessore*—figure, etc.

*Meyer-Heine*—figure and ornaments on enamel.

*Parant*—figure, etc.

*Philip*—decorator on enamel.

*Schilt, Abel*—figure, subjects, portraits.

*Solon, Dlle.*—figure, subjects.

*Treverret, Dlle. de*—figure.

*Van Os*—flowers and fruits.

*Van Marck*—landscape.

# MARKS USED AT SEVRES TO INDICATE
# DATES OF MANUFACTURE

| | | | | |
|---|---|---|---|---|
| A (Vincennes) | . . . . . . . 1753 | N | . . . . . . . . . . . . 1766 |
| B " | . . . . . . . 1754 | O | . . . . . . . . . . . . 1767 |
| C " | . . . . . . . . 1755 | P | . . . . . . . . . . . . 1768 |
| D | . . . . . . . . . . . . 1756 | Q | . . . . . . . . . . . . 1769 |
| E | . . . . . . . . . . . . 1757 | R | . . . . . . . . . . . . 1770 |
| F | . . . . . . . . . . . . 1758 | S | . . . . . . . . . . . . 1771 |
| G | . . . . . . . . . . . . 1759 | T | . . . . . . . . . . . . 1772 |
| H | . . . . . . . . . . . . 1760 | U | . . . . . . . . . . . . 1773 |
| I | . . . . . . . . . . . . 1761 | V | . . . . . . . . . . . . 1774 |
| J | . . . . . . . . . . . . 1762 | X | . . . . . . . . . . . . 1775 |
| K | . . . . . . . . . . . . 1763 | Y | . . . . . . . . . . . . 1776 |
| L | . . . . . . . . . . . . 1764 | Z | . . . . . . . . . . . . 1777 |
| M | . . . . . . . . . . . . 1765 | | |

| | | | | |
|---|---|---|---|---|
| AA | . . . . . . . . . . . 1778 | JJ | . . . . . . . . . . . . 1787 |
| BB | . . . . . . . . . . . 1779 | KK | . . . . . . . . . . . . 1788 |
| CC | . . . . . . . . . . . 1780 | LL | . . . . . . . . . . . . 1789 |
| DD | . . . . . . . . . . . 1781 | MM | . . . . . . . . . . . . 1790 |
| EE | . . . . . . . . . . . 1782 | NN | . . . . . . . . . . . . 1791 |
| FF | . . . . . . . . . . : 1783 | OO | . . . . . . . . . . . 1792 |
| GG | . . . . . . . . . . . 1784 | PP | . . . . . . . . . . . 1793 |
| HH | . . . . . . . . . . . 1785 | QQ | . . . . . . . . . . . . 1794 |
| II | . . . . . . . . . . . 1786 | RR | . . . . . . . . . . . . 1795 |

# MARKS ON PORCELAIN OF FRANCE

# MARKS ON PORCELAIN OF
# GERMANY, ETC.

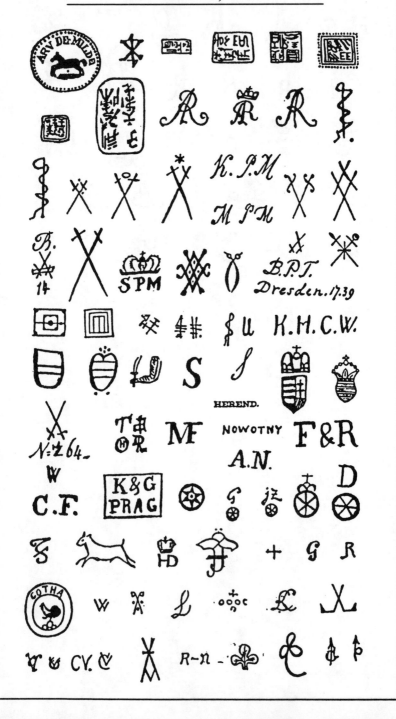

# MARKS ON POTTERY AND
# PORCELAIN OF ENGLAND

# MARKS ON POTTERY OF
# THE UNITED STATES

## PENNSYLVANIA POTTERIES

 P   H R  Henry Roudebush
April ‖ 28th 1811

  CH  AH  PM

IT  Johan Drny 1809  H.T. IS.T.

 Willoughby Smith
Wumelsdorf

William Ellis Tucker
China Manufacturer
Philadelphia
1825

Tucker & Hulme
China Manufacturer
Philadelphia
AM

Tucker & Hulme
Philadelphia
1828

Manufactured
by Jos Hemphill
Philadw

W  W  m  F  H  V  CB

RALPH B. BEECH
PATENTED
JUNE 5, 1851
KENSINGTON, PA.

K & S  Y  Phoenix POttery

  ETRUSCAN
ETRUSCAN MAJOLICA

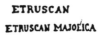  C.PCo
LTD

CPCo
LTD

Galloway & Graff
Philadelphia.

    S.E.T.
CO.

HR    MORAVIAN  MORAVIAN

# NEW JERSEY POTTERIES

AMERICAN POTT'S CO
JERSEY CITY

R. & T

W.M.CO.

BELLEEK

GREENWOOD CHINA
TRENTON, N.J.

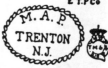

E T.P.Co

M.A.P.
TRENTON.

M.A.P.
TRENTON
N.J.

M
CHINA
L

WARRANTED

HABBEN
PATERSON,
N.J.

TRILBY
J. M. & S. CO.

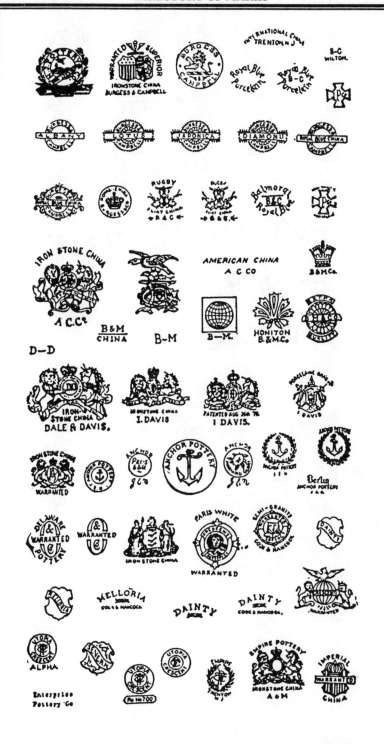

# NEW YORK POTTERIES

A-R

# NEW ENGLAND POTTERIES

  Nichols & Alford Manufacturers 1854 Burlington Vt

   K C A W CHELSEA KERAMIC ART WORKS ROBERTSON & SONS

N.M.P.CO.  NMPCo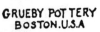

GRUEBY POTTERY BOSTON.U.S.A    GRUEBY BOSTON.MASS

RE E.R.F M.S GRUEBY

MERRIMAC CERAMIC COMPANY

MERRIMAC

W.P. P

N P S Æ

A

# OHIO POTTERIES

SICARDO WELLER.

TURADA WELLER

OWENS UTOPIAN

HENRI DEUX

OWENS FEROZA

A.E.T. Cº

La Francaise Porcelain

Xenneth

Greek

PORCELAIN

KOKUS CHINA

VENUS PORCELAIN

COLUMBIA

LAFAYETTE PORCELAIN

REVERE

PORCELAIN

EXTRA QUALITY STONE CHINA

WARRANTED

Guernsey.

CAMBRIDGE

OAKWOOD

Acorn

Thomas China Co

EXTRA QUALITY STONE CHINA

WARRANTED

THE BELL POTTERY CO
FINDLAY OHIO

BELL CHINA,
B P Co
Findlay Ohio

# SOUTHERN POTTERIES

 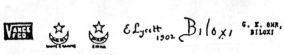 

# WESTERN POTTERIES

PEORIA
ILLINOIS

HOTEL
← J P Co.

JEWEL
C.P.Co

REGINA
C.P. CO.

ALMA

HOBSON

C P CO.
ROYAL

C.P. CO.
REX

·HELEN.

CROWN HOTEL
WARE

Crown
Porcelain.

RENA.

ROBLIN

ROBLIN

M C P

# PRIVATE MARKS OF
# ROOKWOOD DECORATORS

A.R.V.   A·M·B·   C·J·D·    H·R·S·    M·H·S·

A.H.   A·G     J·A·   WHB   S·L·   JTF

AB   A.D.S     C·F·B·   I·B·     S·S·   L·A·M·

AMB   B—    E·R·F·     W·D   LLL B

C·H   C·C·L      W·P·M·D   M·L·S

a·m·v·    D·C·   E·C·L   J·D·W·     M·L·R

ABS    E·P·C     K·C·M·   W·P·M·D

S    E·P·Z   F·Y·   K   WK·     LR·

ass   C·F·S    C·D·F·   H·W·      N·P   L·N·L·

ABS   C·S·   E·A·   H·H   G·H     m·h·K·

A·V·B   C·A·B   E·B·I·C·   H·E·W·   TOM   J·E·   L·E·H·   S·M·

# MARKS FOUND ON CHINESE WARES

## CHRONOLOGICAL TABLE

| Mark | Transcription | Year of the Cycle | Mark | Transcription | Year of the Cycle | Mark | Transcription | Year of the Cycle |
|---|---|---|---|---|---|---|---|---|
| 子甲 | Chia-tzŭ | 1 | 申甲 | Chia-shĕn | 21 | 辰甲 | Chia-ch'ĕn | 41 |
| 丑乙 | I-ch'ŏu | 2 | 酉乙 | I-yu | 22 | 巳乙 | I-ssŭ | 42 |
| 寅丙 | Ping-yin | 3 | 戌丙 | Ping-hsŭ | 23 | 午丙 | Ping-wu | 43 |
| 卯丁 | Ting-mao | 4 | 亥丁 | Ting-hai | 24 | 未丁 | Ting-wei | 44 |
| 辰戊 | Mou-ch'ĕn | 5 | 子戊 | Mou-tzŭ | 25 | 申戊 | Mou-shĕn | 45 |
| 巳己 | Chi-ssŭ | 6 | 丑己 | Chi-ch'ou | 26 | 酉己 | Chi-yu | 46 |
| 午庚 | Kĕng-wu | 7 | 寅庚 | Kĕng-yin | 27 | 戌庚 | Kĕng-hsŭ | 47 |
| 未辛 | Hsin-wei | 8 | 卯辛 | Hsin-mao | 28 | 亥辛 | Hsin-hai | 48 |
| 申壬 | Jĕn-shĕn | 9 | 辰壬 | Jĕn-ch'ĕn | 29 | 子壬 | Jĕn-tzŭ | 49 |
| 酉癸 | Kuei-yu | 10 | 巳癸 | Kuei-ssŭ | 30 | 丑癸 | Kuei-ch'ou | 50 |
| 戌甲 | Chia-hsŭ | 11 | 午甲 | Chia-wu | 31 | 寅甲 | Chia-yin | 51 |
| 亥乙 | I-hai | 12 | 未乙 | I-wei | 32 | 卯乙 | I-mao | 52 |
| 子丙 | Ping-tzŭ | 13 | 申丙 | Ping-shĕn | 33 | 辰丙 | Ping-ch'ĕn | 53 |
| 丑丁 | Ting-ch'ou | 14 | 酉丁 | Ting-yu | 34 | 巳丁 | Ting-ssŭ | 54 |
| 寅戊 | Mou-yin | 15 | 戌戊 | Mou-hsŭ | 35 | 午戊 | Mou-wu | 55 |
| 卯己 | Chi-mao | 16 | 亥己 | Chi-hai | 36 | 未己 | Chi-wei | 56 |
| 辰庚 | Kĕng-ch'ĕn | 17 | 子庚 | Kĕng-tzŭ | 37 | 申庚 | Kĕng-shĕn | 57 |
| 巳辛 | Hsin-ssŭ | 18 | 丑辛 | Hsin-ch'ou | 38 | 酉辛 | Hsin-yu | 58 |
| 午壬 | Jĕn-wu | 19 | 寅壬 | Jĕn-yin | 39 | 戌壬 | Jĕn-hsŭ | 59 |
| 未癸 | Kuei-wei | 20 | 卯癸 | Kuei-mao | 40 | 亥癸 | Kuei-hai | 60 |

# MARKS, INSCRIPTIONS AND CHINESE CHARACTERS

| 甲 chia | 乙 i | 丙 ping | 丁 ting | 戊 mou | 己 chi | 庚 keng | 辛 hsin | 壬 jen | 癸 kuei |
|---|---|---|---|---|---|---|---|---|---|
| 子 [1] | 丑 [2] | 寅 [3] | 卯 [4] | 辰 [5] | 巳 [6] | 午 [7] | 未 [8] | 申 [9] | 酉 [10] |
| 戌 [11] | 亥 [12] | 子 [13] | 丑 [14] | 寅 [15] | 卯 [16] | 辰 [17] | 巳 [18] | 午 [19] | 未 [20] |
| 申 [21] | 酉 [22] | 戌 [23] | 亥 [24] | 子 [25] | 丑 [26] | 寅 [27] | 卯 [28] | 辰 [29] | 巳 [30] |
| 午 [31] | 未 [32] | 申 [33] | 酉 [34] | 戌 [35] | 亥 [36] | 子 [37] | 丑 [38] | 寅 [39] | 卯 [40] |
| 辰 [41] | 巳 [42] | 午 [43] | 未 [44] | 申 [45] | 酉 [46] | 戌 [47] | 亥 [48] | 子 [49] | 丑 [50] |
| 寅 [51] | 卯 [52] | 辰 [53] | 巳 [54] | 午 [55] | 未 [56] | 申 [57] | 酉 [58] | 戌 [59] | 亥 [60] |

# CHRONOLOGICAL GUIDE

| | | |
|---|---|---|
| 一二三四五六七八九十 | 1 2 3 4 5 6 7 8 9 10 | |
| 五十六 | 36 | |
| 一年 | | 1. Year |
| 元年 | | |
| 九年六月十日 | | 9. Year 6. Month 10. Day |
| 百 千 萬 | 100 1000 10000 | |
| 春夏秋冬 | | Spring Summer Autumn Winter |
| 十二 | 12 | |
| 二十 | 20 | |
| 年 歲 月 日 | | Year Year Month Day |

# NIEN-HAOS OF THE MING DYNASTY

年 洪
製 武

Hung-wu
(1368–1398)

年 永 樂
製 樂

Yung-lo
(1403–1424)

德 大
年 明
製 宣

Hsüan-tê (1426–1435)

化 大
年 明
製 成

年 成
製 化

成化

Ch'êng-hua (1465–1487)

治 大
年 明
製 弘

Hung-chih
(1488–1505)

德 大
年 明
製 正

Chêng-tê
(1506–1521)

靖 大
年 明
製 嘉

Chia-ching
(1522–1566)

慶 大
年 明
製 隆

Lung-ch'ing
(1567–1572)

曆 大
年 明
製 萬

Wan-li
(1573–1619)

啟 大
年 明
製 天

T'ien-ch'i
(1621–1627)

年 崇
製 禎

Ch'ung-chêng
(1628–1643)

# NIEN-HAOS OF THE CHING DYNASTY

Shun-chiň (1644–1661)

K'ang-hsi (1662–1722)

Yung-chêng (1723–1735)

Ch'ien-lung (1736–1795)

Chia-ch'ing (1796–1820)

Tao-kuang (1821–1850)

Hsien-fêng (1851–1861)

T'ung-chih (1862–1874)

Kuang-hsü (1875–1908)

# MARKS AND SYMBOLS ON POTTERY OF CHINA

Three forms of the two fish mark, found on old blue ware: one of the earliest known, from 969-1106.

The sesamum flower. Various flower marks are found, in ancient and modern periods

Hoa: a small flower inside a cup. Marks the Yung-lo period, 1403-1424.

Butterfly

Show: long life; a wish for longevity, common in one or another of these and other forms on porcelain: some-

Fuh-che: happiness

Luh: wealth

Keih: good luck.

times repeated a hundred or more times. Such pieces are called "hundred show."

Circular show mark.

Oval show mark

Thin form of show

Fuh-che: happiness

Yuh-chin: precious gem.

Wan-yuh: beautiful gem.

Chin-wan: valuable rarity

## MARKS, SYMBOLS, ETC.

Yuh: a gem; precious thing

Wan: literature.

Hing: flourishing.

Ke: a vessel; vase; ability.

Paou: precious.

Ting: perfect

Tsuen: perfect; a name.

King   good wishes

A name.

Woo-fuh: the five blessings —long life, health, riches, love of virtue, a natural death.

Woo-chin: the five blessings.

Chin-yuh: precious gem.

Leen ching khe how (not translated).

Jo shin chin tsang: precious property; Jo shin (name).

Same mark

Same mark.

Ting Khe che she chin paou } Ting of very precious and costly stone.

Ting Khe che yuh chin paou } Same meaning.

Ta-keih: prosperity; good luck.

Choo-foo: a polite expression in China.   Mark used 1260-1367

Keang-tang: preserved ginger   Used 1522-1566.

Tsaou-tang: preserves; chow-chow Used 1522-1566.

Tung-gan, a name.

Yung-ching, a name.

Tsae Jun tang che } Made for the brilliant hall of the middle.

Wei foo ching } Made to add to the jasper.

Jin ho kwan } Hall of brotherhood.

Another form.

A mandarin mark of honor.

The sounding stone.

Another sounding instrument.

Sacred ax.

Shell or helmet?

Shell?

Shell?

Standard table.

## MARKS, SYMBOLS, ETC.

| Mark | Reading | Meaning |
|---|---|---|
| 玉思 雅有 製美 | Yuh Chung, ya yuh, che mei | For the true hearted, elegant gem made. |
| 福壽 如比 東南 海山 | | Long life as the south mountain. Happiness like the east sea. |
| 祥萬 製明 | Wan ming cheang (name) che (made). | |
| 御雍 製正 | Yung ching yu che; made for Yung ching. | |
| 寒先堂 | Fung seen tang | Hall of ancestors |
| 堂奇 製美 | Tang Khe che yuh | Made for hall of wonderful beauty. |
| 堂偵 製德 | Tang Ching che ti | Made for hall of virtuous study. |
| 堂珮 製玉 | Tang Pi che yuh | Made for hall of jeweled girdle. |
| 堂紫 製刺 | Tang Tze che tze | Made for hall of violet embroidery. |
| 堂敬 製畏 | Tang King che wei | Made for hall of worship. |
| 長富 泰貴 佳玉 器堂 | Kea Yuh ke tang | Beautiful vase for hall of gems. |
| | Chang Fuh chun kwei | Wealth, honor, long youth. |
| 長富 命貴 | Chang Fuh ming kwei | Wealth, honor, long life. |
| 賜天 福官 | Tze Teen fuh kwan | Heaven grant happiness. |
| 如奇 玉珍 | Jou Khe woo chin | Wonderful as the five precious things |

Leaves. Frequent marks.

Treasures of writing, stone for ink, brushes for writing, a roll of paper, etc. Found as a mark; and common, as are many of the previous designs, in the surface decorations of porcelains.

Badge of authority; on pieces for mandarins.

Tablet of honor, including the swastika.

Another form of the same.

| Mark | Reading | Meaning |
|---|---|---|
| 如奇 玉珍 | Jou Khe, yuh chin | Wonderful gem, resembling a jewel. |
| 如奇 玉玩 | Jou Khe, yuh wan | Same signification. |
| 雅聖 集友 | Ya Ching, tsei yu | Remarkable meeting of philosophers and friends. |
| 珍博 玩古 | Chin Poo, wan ku | Valuable curiosity for antiquaries. |
| 寶文 玉鼎 | Paou Wan, ting yah | Elegant, perfect, precious ting; metal incense pot. |
| 山文 斗章 | Shan Wan, tow shang | Compliment; comparing to a mountain and the North star |
| 雅美 製玉 | Ya Mei, che yuh | Made for one who knows gems. |
| 萬疆 無壽 | | Wan show woo keang: an unlimited long life |
| | Wan show woo keang | Same. This is in the seal character |
| 皋江 造喝 | | Keang ming kaou (name); tsaou (maker) |

# MARKS, SYMBOLS, ETC.

 Beautiful vase for the wealthy and noble. Otherwise translated: wealth, honors and intellect.

 Probably a name.

 Valuable vase for divining

 These three combinations or arrangements of lines, known as the eight diagrams of Fuhhi, frequently occur on Chinese porcelain. They have reference to certain mystic ideas, utterly unintelligible to us, relating to the genders, the principles of creation, the origin of all things, etc., etc. Chinese philosophers profess to understand their meaning and suggestions, and the Chinese regard them as talismanic.

 Chu shih chü (red rocks retreat).

 Yu chai (quiet pavilion)

Ku yüeh hsuan chih (made by Ku Yueh Hsuan).

Lu i t'ang (hall of green ripples).

Shěn tě t'ang chih (made for the hall of cultivation of virtue).

Ts'ai jun t'ang chih (made in the hall of brilliant colours).

 Ching wei t'ang chih (made for the hall of respectful awe).

Ta ya chai (pavilion of grand culture).

 Bamboo leaves, used as a mark at King-te-chin, 1573-1619. We have also found the leaves used as an exterior decoration of porcelain dishes which we believe to be Persian.

 Square marks, common on old specimens, in these and many other forms.

 Paou: precious

 Chiang ming kao tsao (made by Chiang Ming-kao).

 Ch'ěn kuo chih tsao (made by Ch'ěn Kuo-chih).

 Yu fěng yang lin (Yang-lin of Yu-fěng).

 Pai-shih (white rock) and Ling nan hui chě (Canton picture).

 Wang tso t'ing tso (made by Wang Tso-t'ing).

 Wang ping jung tso (made by Wang Ping-jung).

## MARKS, SYMBOLS, ETC.

 f Chao-chin.

 Chung t'un shih (Chung-t'un family).

 Chih (made to command).

 Shop marks.

 Li-chih.

 Lai-kuan.

 Ch'i yü pao ting chih chêo (a gem among precious vessels of rare jade).

 Chao tsung ho yin (seal of Ho Chao-tsung).

 Ko Ming hsiang chih (made by Ko Ming-hsiang).

 Chên wan (precious trinket).

 Ko yüan hsiang chih (made by Ko Yuan-hsiang).

 Yü (jade).

 Yi hsing tzŭ sha (brown earth of Yi-hsing).

 Ya wan (elegant trinket).

 G mark.

 Ch'üan (complete).

 Fu (happiness).

 Chi (good luck).

 Lu (rank).

 Shou (longevity)

 Endless knot.

 Spider " mark (a form of shou).

 Ling chih fungus.

 Head of a ju-i sceptre.

 A tripod.

 Fu (an embroidery ornament).

# MARKS FOUND ON JAPANESE POTTERY AND PORCELAIN

## MARKS OF PERIODS

| | | |
|---|---|---|
| 德建 中文 授天 和弘 | Ken-tok, 1370. | |
| | Bun-tin, 1372. | |
| | Ten-du, 1375 | |
| | Ko-wa. 1380 | |
| 中元 四德明 永廉 長正 | Gen-tin, 1380. | |
| | Mei-tok, 1393. | |
| | O-yei, 1394. | |
| | Show-tiyo, 1428. | |
| 享永 吉嘉 安文 德宝 | Yei-kiyo, 1429 | |
| | Ka-kitsu, 1441 | |
| | Bun-an, 1444 | |
| | Ho-tok, 1449 | |
| 德亨 正康 祿長 正寬 | Kiyo-tok, 1452 | |
| | Ko-show, 1455 | |
| | Chiyo-rok, 1457 | |
| | Kwan-show, 1460. | |
| 正文 仁廉 明文 亨延 德明 龍文 | Bun-show, 1466. | |
| | O-nin, 1467. | |
| | Bun-mei, 1469 | |
| | Chiyo-kiyo, 1487. | |
| | En-tok, 1489 | |
| | Mei-o, 1492. | |
| | Bun-ki, 1501 | |

| | | |
|---|---|---|
| 正永 永大 祿亨 永大 | Yei-show, 1504. | |
| | Dai-jei, 1521 | |
| | Kiyo-rok, 1528 | |
| | Di-yei, 1532 | |
| 治弘 祿永 元 | Ko-dsi, 1555. | |
| | Yei-rok, 1558 | |
| | Gen-ki, 1570. | |
| 正天 祿文 長慶 和元 | Ten-show, 1573 | |
| | Bun-rok, 1592 | |
| | Kei-chiyo, 1596. | |
| | Gen-wa, 1615 | |
| 永寬 保正 安慶 應承 | Kwan-jei, 1624. | |
| | Show-ho, 1644. | |
| | Kei-an, 1648. | |
| | Show-o, 1652. | |
| 曆明 治萬 文寬 寬延 | Mei-reki, 1655. | |
| | Man-dsi, 1658. | |
| | Kwan-bun, 1661. | |
| | Yen-po, 1673 | |
| 和天 辛貞 祿元 永寶 | Ten-wa, 1681 | |
| | Tei-kiyo, 1684. | |
| | Gen-rok, 1688. | |
| | Ho-yei, 1704. | |

| | | |
|---|---|---|
| 德正 保享 文元 保寬 | Show-tok, 1711. | |
| | Kiyo-ho, 1717 | |
| | Gen-bun, 1736. | |
| | Kwan-po, 1741. | |
| 享延 延寬 曆寶 和明 | Yen-kiyo, 1744. | |
| | Kwan-jen, 1748. | |
| | Ho-reki, 1751. | |
| | Mei-wa, 1764. | |
| 永安 明天 政寬 和享 | An-jei, 1772. | |
| | Ten-mei, 1781. | |
| | Kwan-sei, 1789. | |
| | Kiyo-wa, 1801. | |
| 化文 政文 保天 化弘 | Bun-kwa, 1804. | |
| | Bun-sei, 1818. | |
| | Ten-po, 1834. | |
| | Ko-kua, 1844. | |
| 永嘉 久文 治元 廉慶 | Ka-yei, 1848. | |
| | Bun-se, 1854. | |
| | Man-yen, 1860. | |
| | Bun-kin, 1861. | |
| 治明 政安 延萬 | Gen-di, 1861 | |
| | Kei-o, 1865. | |
| | Mei-di, 1868. | |

## ENAMEL MARKS

} Enamel mark. Forgery ? of Chinese date 1645.

} Di-Nipon: Great Japan

Han-suki, maker. (Enamel.)

} Nipon: Japan. Next signs illegible.

Eurok, maker. (Enamel.)

## BANKO POTTERIES

Nipon, Japan.

Ari-nori, name.

Banko.

Shing-en, a name

Banko.

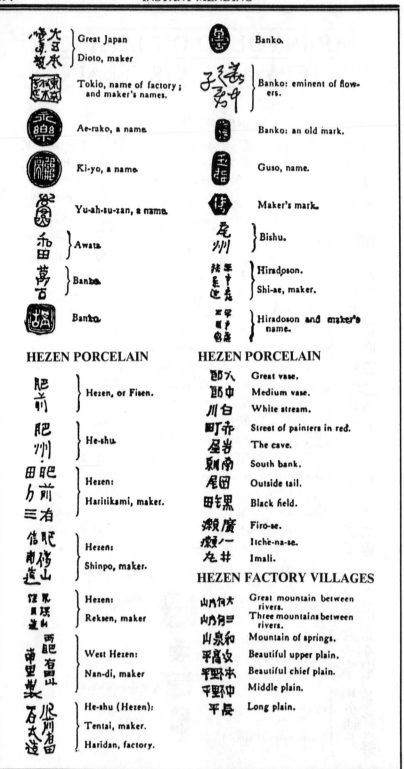

Great Japan

Dioto, maker

Tokio, name of factory; and maker's names.

Ae-rako, a name.

Ki-yo, a name.

Yu-ah-su-zan, a name.

} Awata

} Banka

Banko

Banko.

} Banko: eminent of flowers.

Banko: an old mark.

Guso, name.

Maker's mark.

} Bishu.

Hiradoson.

Shi-ae, maker.

} Hiradoson and maker's name.

## HEZEN PORCELAIN

} Hezen, or Fisen.

} He-shu

Hezen:

Haritikami, maker.

Hezen:

Shinpo, maker.

Hezen:

Reksen, maker

West Hezen:

Nan-di, maker

He-shu (Hezen):

Tentai, maker.

Haridan, factory.

## HEZEN PORCELAIN

Great vase.

Medium vase.

White stream.

Street of painters in red.

The cave.

South bank.

Outside tail.

Black field.

Firo-se.

Itchie-na-se.

Imali.

## HEZEN FACTORY VILLAGES

Great mountain between rivers.

Three mountains between rivers.

Mountain of springs.

Beautiful upper plain.

Beautiful chief plain.

Middle plain.

Long plain.

## KAGA POTTERY AND PORCELAIN

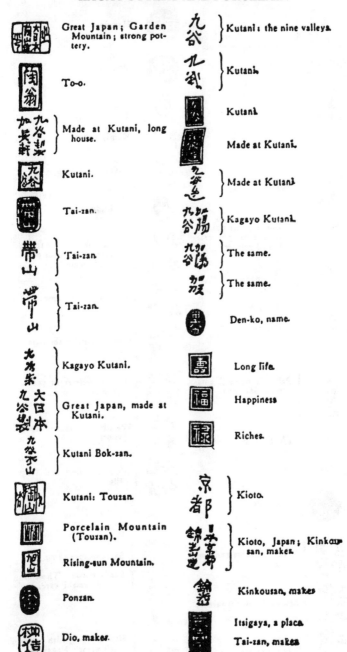

| | |
|---|---|
| | Great Japan; Garden Mountain; strong pottery. |
| | To-o. |
| | Made at Kutani, long house. |
| | Kutani. |
| | Tai-zan. |
| | Tai-zan. |
| | Tai-zan. |
| | Kagayo Kutani. |
| | Great Japan, made at Kutani. |
| | Kutani Bok-zan. |
| | Kutani: Touzan. |
| | Porcelain Mountain (Touzan). |
| | Rising-sun Mountain. |
| | Ponzan. |
| | Dio, maker. |

| | |
|---|---|
| | Kutani: the nine valleys. |
| | Kutani. |
| | Kutani. |
| | Made at Kutani. |
| | Made at Kutani. |
| | Kagayo Kutani. |
| | The same. |
| | The same. |
| | Den-ko, name. |
| | Long life. |
| | Happiness. |
| | Riches. |
| | Kioto. |
| | Kioto, Japan; Kinkousan, maker. |
| | Kinkousan, maker. |
| | Itsigaya, a place. |
| | Tai-zan, maker. |

## SHIBA (TOKEI) POTTERY

## MARKS, SYMBOLS, ETC.

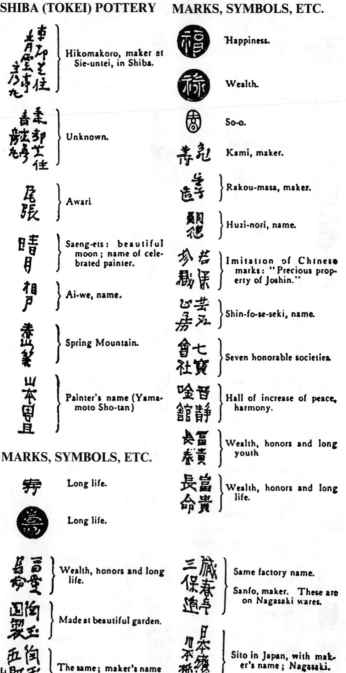

Hikomakoro, maker at Sie-untei, in Shiba.

Unknown.

Awari.

Saeng-ets: beautiful moon; name of celebrated painter.

Ai-we, name.

Spring Mountain.

Painter's name (Yamamoto Sho-tan)

## MARKS, SYMBOLS, ETC.

Long life.

Long life.

Wealth, honors and long life.

Made at beautiful garden.

The same; maker's name (Gos-ki) added.

Happiness.

Wealth.

So-o.

Kami, maker.

Rakou-masa, maker.

Huzi-nori, name.

Imitation of Chinese marks: "Precious property of Joshin."

Shin-fo-se-seki, name.

Seven honorable societies.

Hall of increase of peace, harmony.

Wealth, honors and long youth

Wealth, honors and long life.

Same factory name.

Sanfo, maker. These are on Nagasaki wares.

Sito in Japan, with maker's name; Nagasaki.

## MARKS, SYMBOLS, ETC.

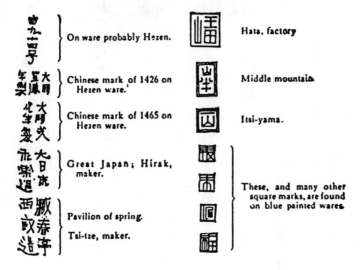

On ware probably Hizen.

Chinese mark of 1426 on Hizen ware.'

Chinese mark of 1465 on Hizen ware.

Great Japan; Hirak, maker.

Pavilion of spring.

Tsi-tze, maker.

Hata, factory

Middle mountain

Itsi-yama.

These, and many other square marks, are found on blue painted wares.

## PLACE-MARKS ON JAPANESE STONEWARE

| 1. Hirado | 2. Kyōto | 3. Kutani | 4. Kutani (Fuku) | 5. Seto |
|-----------|----------|-----------|------------------|---------|
| | | | | |

## FACTORY-MARKS AND SIGNATURES OF ARTISTS
## ON JAPANESE PORCELAIN

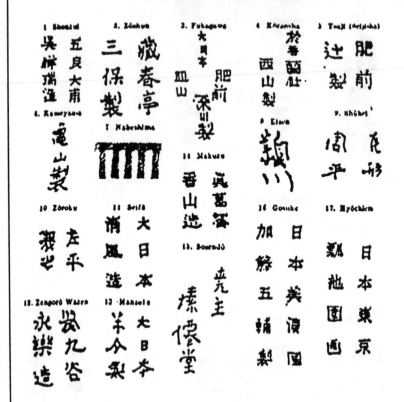

## SIGNATURES OF ARTISTS ON JAPANESE STONEWARE, ETC.

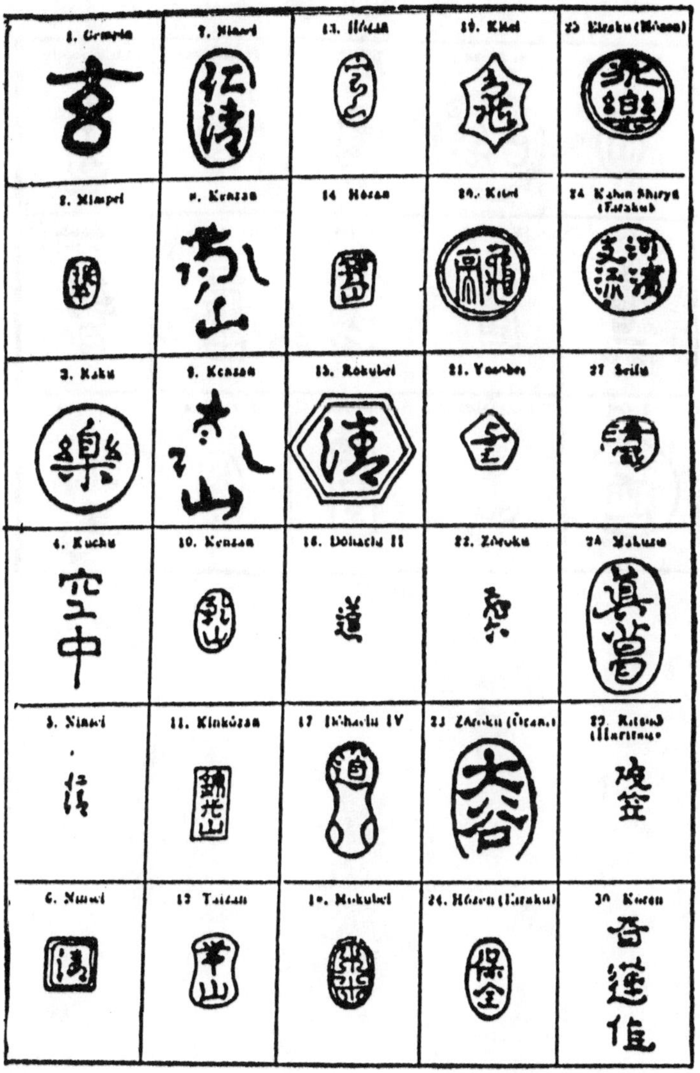

# PLACE-MARKS ON JAPANESE PORCELAIN

# NOTES

# NOTES

# INDEX